FAVORITE BRAND NAME
CHICKEN
COLLECTION

PUBLICATIONS INTERNATIONAL, LTD.

Pictured on the front cover: *Top row, left to right:* Magically Moist Chicken (*page 63*), Savory Orange Chicken (*page 194*) and Chicken Taquitos (*page 157*). *Bottom row, left to right:* Tropical Chicken Salad (*page 35*), Sweet and Spicy Chicken Barbecue (*page 165*) and Calico Chicken Soup (*page 45*).

Pictured on the back cover: *Top row, left to right*: Chicken with Potatoes & Peppers (*page 75*), Shantung Chicken (*page 139*) and Honey 'n' Spice Chicken Kabobs (*page 161*). *Bottom row, left to right*: Polynesian Chicken (*page 143*), Ginger Spicy Chicken (*page 98*) and Ranch Buffalo Wings (*page 8*).

Microwave ovens vary in wattage and power output; cooking times given with microwave directions in this publication may need to be adjusted. Consult manufacturer's instructions for suitable microwave-safe cooking dishes.

Contents

BASICS FOR SUCCESS

Few foods grace the dinner table more often than chicken. Economical, versatile and readily available, chicken is the perfect ingredient for everyday cooking. Plus, chicken is high in protein and low in fat and cholesterol. Its delicious flavor makes it a winning choice for healthy eating.

The following information will help make selecting and preparing chicken a cinch. Be sure to check out all the useful tips and suggestions to make the most of this popular food.

SELECTION

Types of Chicken

Chickens are classified by age and weight. Young chickens are tender and cook quickly; older chickens need slow cooking to make them tender. For best results, it's important to know which type of chicken to buy.

Broiler-fryers are young chickens weighing from 1½ to 3½ pounds. Only 7 to 10 weeks old, they yield tender, mildly flavored meat and are best when broiled, fried or roasted.

Roasters are 4- to 6-pound chickens that are 16 weeks old. As the name implies, they are perfect for roasting and rotisserie cooking.

Capons are young, castrated roosters that weigh from 5 to 7 pounds. These richly flavored birds have a higher fat content and yield more meat than roasters.

Stewing hens are adult chickens from 1 to 1½ years old. They weigh from 4½ to 7 pounds and have tough, stringy meat. Stewing hens are excellent for stocks, soups or stews, since moist-heat preparation tenderizes them and enhances their chicken-y flavor.

What's Available

Supermarkets fulfill a constant demand for chicken with a variety of chicken cuts and products. Here are some of the more popular choices:

Whole chickens of every type are readily available; usually they come with the neck and giblets wrapped separately and stuffed inside. **Livers** and **giblets** can also be found packaged separately for use in stuffings, soups and specialty dishes.

Cut-up chickens, usually broiler-fryers, are disjointed whole chickens consisting of two breast halves, two thighs, two wings and two drumsticks. Small broiler-fryers also come in **halves** and **quarters.**

Chicken pieces are available to suit many needs. **Chicken legs** are whole broiler-fryer legs with the thighs and drumsticks attached. **Thighs** and **drumsticks** are cut-apart chicken legs that are packaged separately. **Wings** are also sold separately. **Drumettes** are disjointed wing sections. **Chicken breasts** are popular because of their tender, meaty, sweet character. They are available whole or split into halves. (*Note:* Recipes in this book that call for chicken breasts refer to one *whole* breast or *both* breast halves, not just one half.)

Boneless skinless chicken has become a favorite choice for today's busy cook because of its convenience and quick-cooking appeal. Boneless breasts, also called **cutlets** or **supremes**, plus **chicken tenders** and boneless thighs are some of the boneless cuts of chicken available.

Ground chicken is a recent addition to the poultry case; its most popular use is as a low-fat replacement for ground beef or pork. Processed chicken includes **canned chunk chicken**, newly introduced chicken **sausage**, chicken **franks** and traditional **deli** and **luncheon meats.**

How to Inspect Chicken

Most chicken sold at supermarkets has been government-inspected for wholesomeness and is usually rated Grade A by the U.S.D.A. Beyond these signs of quality, it's important to check for secure, unbroken packaging. Look for a "sell-by" date stamp on the package as well, which indicates the last day the chicken should be sold.

You should also visually inspect chicken before buying it. The skin should be creamy white to deep yellow; meat should never look gray or pasty.

Check the chicken for odors; they could signal spoilage. After opening a package of chicken, if you notice a strong, unpleasant odor, leave it open on the counter for a few minutes. Sometimes oxidation takes place inside the package, resulting in a slight, but harmless odor. If the odor remains, return the chicken in its package to the store for a refund.

Buying Chicken

Chicken is both economical and convenient. If you purchase whole chickens on sale and cut them apart at home, you can save money. You can save time by stocking your freezer with boneless skinless chicken, which defrosts and cooks quickly. When purchasing chicken, the key is to know what you plan to use it for and buy according to your needs.

PREPARATION

Handling Chicken

When handling raw chicken, you must keep everything that comes into contact with it clean. Raw chicken should be rinsed and patted dry with paper towels before cooking, cutting boards and knives must be washed in hot sudsy water after using and hands must be scrubbed thoroughly before and after handling. Why? Raw chicken can harbor harmful salmonella bacteria. If bacteria are transferred to work surfaces, utensils or hands, they could contaminate other foods as well as the cooked chicken and cause food poisoning. With careful handling and proper cooking, this is easily prevented.

Chicken should always be cooked completely before eating. You should never cook chicken partially, then store it to be finished later, since this promotes bacterial growth.

Cooking Chicken

There are a number of ways to determine if chicken is thoroughly cooked and ready to eat. For whole chickens, a meat thermometer inserted into the thickest part of the thigh, but not near the bones or fat, should register 180°F to 185°F before removing from the oven. If a whole chicken is stuffed, insert the thermometer into the center of the body cavity; when the stuffing registers 160°F, the chicken should be done. (*Note:* Chicken should only be stuffed *just before* roasting; *never* stuff a chicken ahead of time.) Roasted whole chicken breasts are done when they register 170°F on a meat thermometer.

To test bone-in chicken pieces, you should be able to insert a fork into the chicken with ease and the juices should run clear; however, the meat and juices nearest the bones might still be a little pink even though the chicken is cooked thoroughly. Boneless chicken pieces are done when the centers are no longer pink; you can determine this by simply cutting into the chicken with a knife.

To prevent spoilage of cooked chicken or any other cooked foods, never let them stand at room temperature for more than two hours. In hot weather, cooked food should not stand at room temperature for more than one hour.

Storing Chicken

Fresh, raw chicken can be stored in its original wrap for up to two days in the coldest part of the refrigerator. You can freeze chicken in its original packaging safely for up to two months; if you plan to freeze it longer, consider double-wrapping or rewrapping with freezer paper, aluminum foil or plastic wrap. Airtight packaging is the key to freezing chicken successfully.

Freeze chicken immediately if you do not plan to use it within three days after purchasing. When freezing whole chickens, remove and rinse giblets (if any) and pat dry with paper towels. Trim away any excess fat. Tightly wrap, label, date and freeze both chicken and giblets in separate freezer-strength plastic, paper or foil wraps. Repeat this procedure for freezing chicken pieces. However, try storing them in smaller packages in efficient, meal-size portions; this way, defrosting time is reduced because you only thaw what you need.

Thaw frozen chicken, wrapped, in the refrigerator for best results. Thawing times for frozen chicken vary depending on how thoroughly frozen the chicken is and whether the chicken is whole or cut up. A general guideline is to allow 24 hours thawing time for a 5-pound whole chicken; allow about 5 hours per pound for thawing chicken pieces. Never thaw chicken on the kitchen counter; this promotes bacterial growth.

See page 160 for information about grilling and marinating chicken.

Basic Techniques

- **Flattening boneless chicken breasts:** Place one chicken breast half between two sheets of waxed paper. Using the flat side of a meat mallet or rolling pin, gently pound the chicken to desired thickness.
- **Skinning chicken:** Freeze chicken until it is firm, but not hard. Grasp the skin with a clean cotton towel and pull away from meat; discard skin. When finished skinning chicken, launder towel before using again.
- **Disjointing a whole chicken:** See directions with photographs on page 7.

TIPS FOR SUCCESS

- As a rule, two whole chicken breasts (about 12 ounces each) yield about 2 cups chopped cooked chicken; one broiler-fryer (about 3 pounds) yields about 2¹/₂ cups chopped cooked chicken.
- One broiler-fryer (2 to 3 pounds), cut up, makes 3 to 5 servings; one roaster (3 to 6 pounds) makes 4 to 8 servings. One whole chicken breast (about 12 ounces) makes 2 servings; one pound of chicken thighs or drumsticks makes 2 servings.
- For crispy fried chicken, use a shallow skillet; this allows steam to escape and the chicken will become more crispy as a result. Also, fry chicken with the skin side down first so that the fat from the skin will cook itself out; make sure to turn chicken halfway through cooking time for even browning.
- Broil chicken 5 to 6 inches from heat for the best results. Also, serve broiled chicken immediately. If kept warm in the oven, it dries out; if kept warm in a covered dish, it becomes soggy.
- Use your microwave oven to cook boneless skinless chicken breasts for use in recipes that call for chopped cooked chicken. Cook 1 pound of boneless skinless chicken breasts, covered, at HIGH 7 to 8 minutes. Test for doneness; if chicken is still pink, microwave at one-minute intervals until it is no longer pink in center.
- For directions for defrosting chicken in the microwave, consult your microwave oven manufacturer's manual.

Disjointing a Whole Chicken

1. Place chicken, breast side up, on cutting board. Cut between thigh and body of chicken down to hip joint. Bend leg back slightly to free hip joint from socket; cut through hip joint and remove leg. Repeat to remove other leg.

2. To separate drumstick from thigh, place leg on cutting board. Locate joint by moving thigh back and forth with one hand while holding drumstick with other hand. Cut completely through joint. Repeat with other leg.

3. Place chicken on side. Pull one wing out from body; cut through shoulder joint. Turn chicken over and repeat to remove other wing.

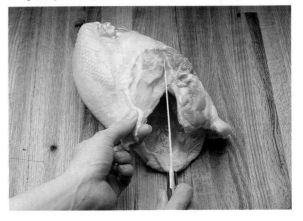

4. Working from tail toward neck, cut through skin connecting breast to backbone, cutting through small rib bones and along outside of collarbone.

5. Turn chicken over and repeat procedure on other side of chicken. Cut through any remaining connective tissue, if necessary; pull breast away from backbone.

6. Place breast, skin side up, on cutting board. Split breast into halves by cutting along one side of breastbone.

FOR STARTERS

A treasury of tasty appetizers! Deluxe Fajita Nachos and Zesty Liver Pâté offer versatile appeal. Try Buffalo-Style Chicken Wings for a popular snack.

Ranch Buffalo Wings

½ cup butter or margarine, melted
¼ cup hot pepper sauce
3 tablespoons vinegar
24 chicken wing drumettes
1 package (1 ounce)
    HIDDEN VALLEY RANCH®
    Milk Recipe Original Ranch®
    Salad Dressing Mix
½ teaspoon paprika
1 cup prepared
    HIDDEN VALLEY RANCH®
    Original Ranch® Salad Dressing
    Celery sticks

Preheat oven to 350°F. In small bowl, whisk together butter, hot pepper sauce and vinegar. Dip drumettes in butter mixture; arrange in single layer in large baking pan. Sprinkle with salad dressing mix. Bake until chicken is browned, 30 to 40 minutes. Sprinkle with paprika. Serve with prepared salad dressing and celery sticks.

Serves 6 to 8 as an appetizer

Southwest Chicken Fingers

⅔ cup HELLMANN'S® or
    BEST FOODS® Real, Light or
    Cholesterol Free Reduced
    Calorie Mayonnaise
⅓ cup prepared salsa
2 boneless skinless chicken breasts,
    cut into 3×1-inch strips
    (about 1¼ pounds)

In large bowl, combine mayonnaise and salsa; set aside 6 tablespoons. Add chicken strips to remaining mayonnaise mixture in large bowl; toss well. Marinate in refrigerator 30 minutes. Grill chicken, 5 inches from heat, turning once, for 4 minutes until chicken is no longer pink in center. Or broil, without turning, 5 inches from heat. Serve with reserved 6 tablespoons mayonnaise mixture.

Makes 6 to 8 appetizer servings

Ranch Buffalo Wings

Cajun-Style Chicken Nuggets

Cajun-Style Chicken Nuggets

　1 envelope LIPTON® Onion or
　　Onion-Mushroom Recipe
　　Soup Mix
　½ cup plain dry bread crumbs
　1½ teaspoons chili powder
　1 teaspoon ground cumin
　1 teaspoon dried thyme leaves
　¼ teaspoon ground red pepper
　2 pounds boneless skinless chicken
　　breasts, cut into 1-inch pieces
　　Vegetable oil

In large bowl, mix onion recipe soup
mix, bread crumbs, chili powder, cumin,
thyme and ground red pepper. Dip
chicken in bread crumb mixture, coating
well.

In large skillet, heat ½ inch oil. Cook
chicken over medium heat, turning
once, until no longer pink in center;
drain on paper towels. Serve warm with
assorted mustards, if desired.

Makes about 5 dozen nuggets

Microwave Directions: Coat chicken as
directed. In 13×9-inch microwave-safe
baking dish, arrange chicken; drizzle
with 2 to 3 tablespoons oil. Microwave,
uncovered, at HIGH 6 minutes or until
chicken is no longer pink in center,
rearranging chicken once; drain on
paper towels. Serve as directed.

Mexican Appetizer Cheesecake

　3 (8-ounce) packages cream cheese,
　　softened
　2 teaspoons WYLER'S® or STEERO®
　　Chicken-Flavor Instant Bouillon
　1½ teaspoons chili powder
　½ teaspoon hot pepper sauce
　2 eggs
　½ cup *hot* water
　1 cup finely chopped cooked
　　chicken
　1 (4-ounce) can chopped green
　　chilies, well drained
　　Salsa, shredded cheese and sliced
　　green onions
　　LA FAMOUS® Tortilla Chips

Preheat oven to 325°F. In large mixer
bowl, beat cream cheese, bouillon, chili
powder and hot pepper sauce until
smooth. Add eggs and water; mix well.
Stir in chicken and chilies. Pour into 9-
inch springform pan. Bake 30 minutes
or until set; cool 15 minutes. Carefully
run knife around edge of pan; remove
side of pan. Top with salsa, cheese and
green onions. Serve warm or chilled
with tortilla chips. Refrigerate leftovers.

Makes 10 to 12 appetizer servings

Cold Yogurt Soup

1 cup finely chopped cooked
    chicken
1 teaspoon lemon juice
3/4 teaspoon minced fresh dill *or*
    1/4 teaspoon dried dill weed
1/2 teaspoon salt
1/8 teaspoon garlic powder
    Pinch white pepper
2 cups plain yogurt
1 small cucumber, seeded and diced
1/3 cup chopped celery
3 tablespoons thinly sliced green
    onions
    Fresh dill sprigs for garnish

Place chicken, lemon juice, minced dill, salt, garlic powder and pepper in small bowl; toss lightly. Cover; refrigerate 30 minutes.

Place yogurt in medium bowl. Stir with fork or wire whisk until smooth and creamy. Stir chicken mixture, cucumber, celery and onions into yogurt. Pour soup into serving bowls; garnish with dill sprigs.   *Makes 4 appetizer servings*

Cold Yogurt Soup

Deluxe Fajita Nachos

2½ cups shredded cooked chicken
1 package (1.27 ounces) LAWRY'S®
   Spices & Seasonings for Fajitas
⅓ cup water
8 ounces tortilla chips
1¼ cups (5 ounces) shredded Cheddar
   cheese
1 cup (4 ounces) shredded Monterey
   Jack cheese
1 large tomato, chopped
1 can (2¼ ounces) sliced pitted ripe
   olives, drained
¼ cup sliced green onions
   Prepared salsa

In medium skillet, combine chicken,
Spices & Seasonings for Fajitas and
water; blend well. Bring to a boil;
reduce heat and simmer 3 minutes. On
large, shallow ovenproof platter, arrange
chips. Top with chicken mixture and
cheeses. Place under broiler to melt
cheeses. Top with tomato, olives, green
onions and salsa.
   Makes 4 appetizer or 2 main-dish servings
Presentation: Garnish with guacamole
and sour cream.

Hint: For a spicier version, add sliced
jalapeños.

Parchment-Wrapped Chicken

2 boneless skinless chicken breasts
   (about 1¼ pounds)
3 tablespoons KIKKOMAN® Soy
   Sauce
1 teaspoon ginger juice*
¼ teaspoon sugar
   Boiling water
½ pound fresh bean sprouts
6 green onions and tops, cut into
   2-inch lengths and slivered
⅓ cup chopped toasted walnuts**

Cut eight 8-inch squares of parchment
paper; set aside. Cut chicken into thin,
narrow strips, about 3 inches long.
Combine soy sauce, ginger juice and
sugar in large bowl; stir in chicken. Let
stand 30 minutes.

Meanwhile, pour boiling water over
bean sprouts to cover; let stand 1
minute. Drain; cool under cold water
and drain well. Thoroughly toss chicken
mixture with bean sprouts, green
onions and walnuts.

Place about ½ cup chicken-bean sprout
mixture in center of each parchment
square. Fold bottom point of parchment
over filling; crease just below filling and
fold point over and under filling. Fold
side points over filling, overlapping
slightly. Crease paper to hold folds. Fold
remaining corner down so point extends
below bottom of bundle; tuck this point
between folded sides. Crease paper to
hold folds. Repeat with remaining
parchment squares and filling.

Place bundles, seam side down, in
single layer on steamer rack. Set rack in
large pot or wok of boiling water. (Do
not allow water level to reach bundles.)
Cover and steam about 7 minutes, or
until chicken is tender. Serve
immediately.

   Makes 8 appetizer servings

*Peel fresh ginger root, then squeeze
through garlic press.

**To toast walnuts, spread nuts in
shallow pan. Bake in preheated 350°F
oven 12 to 15 minutes or until golden
brown, stirring frequently.

Deluxe Fajita Nachos

Garlicky Gilroy Chicken Wings

Garlicky Gilroy Chicken Wings

2 pounds chicken wings (about 15 wings)
3 heads fresh garlic,* separated into cloves and peeled
1 cup plus 1 tablespoon olive oil, divided
10 to 15 drops Tabasco® pepper sauce
1 cup grated Parmesan cheese
1 cup Italian-style bread crumbs
1 teaspoon pepper

Preheat oven to 375°F. Disjoint chicken wings, removing tips. (If desired, save tips to make chicken stock.) Rinse wings; pat dry. Place garlic, 1 cup oil and pepper sauce in blender or food processor container; cover and process until smooth.

Pour garlic mixture into small bowl. Combine cheese, bread crumbs and pepper in shallow dish. Dip wings into garlic mixture, then roll, one at a time, in crumb mixture until thoroughly coated. Brush shallow, nonstick baking pan with remaining 1 tablespoon oil; arrange wings in a single layer. Drizzle remaining garlic mixture over wings; sprinkle with remaining crumb mixture.

Bake 45 to 60 minutes or until browned and crisp. Garnish as desired.
Makes about 6 appetizer servings

*The whole garlic bulb is called a *head*.

*Favorite recipe from **The Fresh Garlic Association***

Stuffed Mushroom Crowns

   2 cans (6 ounces each) cooked-in-
      butter mushroom crowns,
      undrained*
   1 package (3 ounces) cream cheese,
      softened
   ²/₃ cup finely chopped cooked
      chicken
   2 teaspoons lemon juice
   ¹/₈ teaspoon onion powder
   ¹/₈ teaspoon salt
      Pinch pepper
      Pinch garlic powder
      Paprika

Drain mushrooms; reserve crowns.
Remove and finely chop stems.

Combine cream cheese, mushroom
stems, chicken, lemon juice, onion
powder, salt, pepper and garlic powder
in small bowl. Spoon mixture into
hollow of each mushroom crown.
Refrigerate 30 minutes. Sprinkle each
crown with paprika.

Makes about 50 stuffed mushrooms

*If desired, 1 pound small fresh
mushrooms can be substituted for the 2
cans cooked-in-butter mushroom
crowns. Remove and finely chop stems.
Cook mushroom crowns and chopped
stems in 1 to 2 tablespoons butter in
skillet just until browned on rounded
sides, no more than 3 minutes. Proceed
as directed.

Empañaditas

   Chicken Filling (recipe follows)
   Pastry for double-crust 9-inch pie
   1 egg yolk mixed with 1 teaspoon
      water

Preheat oven to 375°F. Prepare Chicken
Filling. Roll out pastry, one half at a
time, on floured board, to ¹/₈-inch
thickness; cut into 2¹/₂-inch circles. Place
about 1 teaspoon Chicken Filling on
each circle. Fold dough over to make
half moons; seal edges with fork. Prick
tops; brush with egg mixture. Place,
slightly apart, on ungreased baking
sheets. Bake 12 to 15 minutes or until
golden brown. Serve warm.

Makes about 3 dozen empañaditas

Chicken Filling

   1 tablespoon butter or margarine
   1 cup finely chopped onion
   2 cups finely chopped cooked
      chicken
   ¹/₄ cup canned diced green chilies
   1 tablespoon capers, rinsed, drained
      and coarsely chopped
   ¹/₄ teaspoon salt
   1 cup (4 ounces) shredded Monterey
      Jack cheese

Melt butter in medium skillet over
medium heat. Add onion; cook until
tender. Stir in chicken, chilies, capers
and salt; cook 1 minute. Remove from
heat and let cool; stir in cheese.

Buffalo-Style Chicken Wings

Vegetable oil
12 chicken wings (about 2 pounds)
½ cup all-purpose flour
2 tablespoons butter or margarine
¼ cup sliced green onions
1 medium clove garlic, finely chopped
1 cup (8 ounces) WISH-BONE® Sweet 'n Spicy® French Dressing
1 teaspoon dried thyme leaves
1 teaspoon dried oregano leaves
1 teaspoon ground cumin
½ teaspoon hot pepper sauce (variations follow)
WISH-BONE® Chunky Blue Cheese Dressing
Celery sticks

In deep-fat fryer or large heavy skillet, heat oil to 375°F.

Cut tips off chicken wings (save tips for soup, if desired). Halve chicken wings at joints. Lightly coat chicken with flour, then carefully drop chicken, a few pieces at a time, into hot oil. Fry, turning occasionally, 15 minutes or until golden brown and tender; drain on paper towels.

Meanwhile, in large skillet, melt butter; cook green onions and garlic over medium heat, stirring occasionally, 3 minutes or until onions are tender. Remove from heat and stir in Sweet 'n Spicy French Dressing, thyme, oregano, cumin and hot pepper sauce. Add chicken; toss to coat. Serve with Chunky Blue Cheese Dressing and celery sticks.   *Makes 24 wings*

Variations
First Alarm Chicken Wings: Add 1 teaspoon hot pepper sauce.

Second Alarm Chicken Wings: Add 1½ teaspoons hot pepper sauce.

Third Alarm Chicken Wings: Add 2 teaspoons hot pepper sauce.

• Also terrific with Wish-Bone® Lite Sweet 'n Spicy French, Russian or Lite Russian Dressing.

Chicken Pizza

2 boneless skinless chicken breasts, cut into 1-inch pieces (about 1¼ pounds)
1 package (8 ounces) refrigerated crescent dinner rolls
¼ cup vegetable oil
1 large onion, sliced into thin rings
1 large green bell pepper, sliced into thin rings
½ pound mushrooms, sliced
½ cup pitted ripe olives, sliced
1 can (10½ ounces) pizza sauce with cheese
1 teaspoon garlic salt
1 teaspoon dried oregano leaves
¼ cup grated Parmesan cheese
2 cups (8 ounces) shredded mozzarella cheese

Preheat oven to 425°F. Separate crescent dough into 8 triangles. Press triangles into lightly oiled 12-inch pizza pan, covering completely. Heat oil in large skillet over medium-high heat. Add chicken, onion rings, green pepper rings, mushrooms and olives. Cook and stir about 5 minutes or until chicken is no longer pink in center. Spread pizza sauce over dough. Spoon chicken mixture evenly over sauce. Sprinkle with garlic salt, oregano and Parmesan cheese. Top with mozzarella cheese. Bake 20 minutes or until crust is golden brown.   *Makes 8 appetizer servings*

*Favorite recipe from **National Broiler Council***

Chicken Pizza

Teriyaki Chicken Wings

Teriyaki Chicken Wings

⅓ cup **REALEMON®** Lemon Juice
    from Concentrate
¼ **cup ketchup**
¼ **cup soy sauce**
¼ **cup vegetable oil**
 2 **tablespoons brown sugar**
¼ **teaspoon garlic powder**
¼ **teaspoon pepper**
 3 **pounds chicken wing drumettes** *or*
    chicken wings, cut at joints and
    wing tips removed

In large, shallow dish or resealable
plastic bag, combine all ingredients
except chicken; mix well. Add chicken.
Cover; marinate in refrigerator 6 hours
or overnight, turning occasionally.

Preheat oven to 375°F. Remove chicken
from marinade; arrange on rack in
aluminum foil-lined, shallow baking
pan. Heat marinade thoroughly. Bake
chicken 40 to 45 minutes, basting
occasionally with marinade. Refrigerate
leftovers.　　*Makes about 3 dozen wings*

Microwave Directions: Prepare chicken
as directed. Divide chicken and
marinade between two 8-inch
microwave-safe dishes. Cover with
waxed paper; cook each dish on 100%
power (high) 12 to 14 minutes or until
tender, rearranging pieces once or
twice.

Suez Appetizers

1 large boneless skinless chicken
    breast, cut into 1-inch pieces
    (about 10 ounces)
1½ slices white sandwich bread
1 egg yolk
1 tablespoon minced fresh parsley
1 tablespoon grated onion
½ teaspoon salt
¼ teaspoon pepper
¼ teaspoon ground cumin
⅛ teaspoon garlic powder
⅛ teaspoon ground turmeric
    Chili Peach Sauce (recipe follows)
⅓ cup all-purpose flour
    Vegetable oil

Place chicken and bread in blender or
food processor container; process until
ground. Place mixture in medium bowl;
mix in egg yolk, parsley, onion, salt,
pepper, cumin, garlic powder and
turmeric. Cover; refrigerate 30 minutes.
Prepare Chili Peach Sauce; set aside.

Shape chicken mixture into balls, using
1 rounded teaspoon of mixture for each
ball; roll in flour to coat.

Heat 1 inch oil in Dutch oven to 350°F.
Fry, six balls at a time, in hot oil until
balls are no longer pink in center, 3 to 4
minutes. Drain on paper towels. Keep
warm in 200°F oven until ready to
serve. Serve balls with wooden
toothpicks and Chili Peach Sauce for
dipping.   *Makes 20 appetizers*

Chili Peach Sauce

½ cup mayonnaise
¼ cup chili sauce
2 tablespoons dry onion soup mix
2 tablespoons peach or apricot jam

Combine all ingredients in 1-quart
saucepan. Cook over low heat just until
hot, but not boiling.   *Makes 1 cup*

Suez Appetizers

Shanghai Party Pleasers

1 can (20 ounces) crushed pineapple
   in juice, undrained
¼ cup firmly packed brown sugar
2 tablespoons cornstarch
   Dash of ground ginger
1 cup water
2 tablespoons margarine
1 pound finely chopped, cooked,
   skinned chicken
¾ cup QUAKER® Oat Bran hot
   cereal, uncooked
⅓ cup plain low fat yogurt
⅓ cup finely chopped water
   chestnuts, drained
⅓ cup sliced green onions
2 tablespoons lite soy sauce
1 egg white, slightly beaten
1 teaspoon ground ginger
½ teaspoon salt (optional)

Drain pineapple, reserving juice. In medium saucepan, combine brown sugar, cornstarch and dash of ginger; mix well. Add combined reserved pineapple juice, water, ¼ cup pineapple and margarine; mix well. Bring to a boil over medium-high heat; reduce heat. Simmer about 1 minute, stirring frequently or until sauce is thickened and clear. Set aside.

Heat oven to 400°F. Lightly spray rack of 13×9-inch baking pan with vegetable oil cooking spray, or oil lightly. Combine chicken, oat bran, yogurt, water chestnuts, onions, soy sauce, egg white, 1 teaspoon ginger, salt and remaining pineapple; mix well. Shape into 1-inch balls. Place on prepared rack. Bake 20 to 25 minutes or until light golden brown. Serve with pineapple sauce; garnish with green onions, if desired.

Makes 2 dozen appetizers

Glazed Ginger Chicken

5 tablespoons KIKKOMAN® Soy
   Sauce
3 tablespoons plum jam
1 tablespoon sesame seed, toasted*
1 tablespoon cornstarch
1 tablespoon minced fresh ginger
1 clove garlic, pressed
8 small chicken thighs (about
   2 pounds)

Cut eight 8-inch squares of aluminum foil; set aside. Combine soy sauce, plum jam, sesame seed, cornstarch, ginger and garlic in small saucepan. Bring to boil over medium heat, stirring constantly. Remove from heat and cool slightly. Stir in thighs, a few at a time, to coat each piece well. Place 1 thigh, skin side up, on each foil square. Divide and spoon remaining sauce evenly over thighs. Fold ends of foil to form bundles; crease and fold down to secure well. Place bundles, seam side up, in single layer on steamer rack. Set rack in large pot or wok of boiling water. (Do not allow water level to reach bundles.) Cover and steam 30 minutes, or until chicken is tender. Garnish as desired. Serve immediately.

Makes 8 appetizer servings

*To toast sesame seed, spread seeds in small skillet. Shake skillet over medium heat 2 minutes or until seeds begins to pop and turn golden.

Shanghai Party Pleasers

Yakitori

3 pounds whole chicken breasts
1 bunch green onions, cut into
    1-inch lengths
1 pound chicken livers, trimmed,
    rinsed and drained
1 cup KIKKOMAN® Soy Sauce
¼ cup sugar
1 tablespoon vegetable oil
2 cloves garlic, pressed
¾ teaspoon ground ginger

Remove skin and bones from chicken, keeping meat in 1 piece; cut into 1-inch lengths. Thread chicken pieces onto metal or bamboo skewers with green onions (spear through sides) and chicken livers. Arrange skewers in large, shallow pan. Blend soy sauce, sugar, oil, garlic and ginger; pour marinade over skewers. Brush each skewer thoroughly with marinade. Cover and refrigerate about 1 hour, turning skewers over occasionally. Reserving marinade, remove skewers and place on rack of broiler pan. Broil 5 inches from heat source 3 minutes on each side, or until chicken is tender; brush with reserved marinade after turning.

Makes 4 dozen skewers

Monte Cristo Sandwiches

⅓ cup HELLMANN'S® or
    BEST FOODS® Real, Light or
    Cholesterol Free Reduced
    Calorie Mayonnaise
¼ teaspoon ground nutmeg
⅛ teaspoon freshly ground pepper
12 slices white bread, crusts removed
6 slices Swiss cheese
6 slices cooked ham
6 slices cooked chicken
2 eggs
½ cup milk

In small bowl, combine mayonnaise, nutmeg and pepper; spread on one side of each bread slice. Arrange cheese, ham and chicken on mayonnaise sides of 6 bread slices; top with remaining bread slices, mayonnaise sides down. Cut sandwiches diagonally into quarters. In small bowl, beat together eggs and milk; dip sandwich quarters into egg mixture. Cook on preheated greased griddle or in skillet, turning once, 4 to 5 minutes or until browned and heated through.

Makes 24 mini sandwiches

Bandito Buffalo Wings

1 package ORTEGA® Taco Seasoning
    Mix
12 chicken wings, split with tips
    removed (about 2 pounds)
½ cup ORTEGA® Thick and Chunky
    Salsa, Green Chile Salsa or
    Picante Sauce

Place seasoning mix in large plastic bag. Add a few chicken wings; shake until well coated. Repeat to coat all pieces. Place in lightly greased baking pan. Bake at 375°F, 35 to 40 minutes or until chicken is tender and juices run clear. Serve hot with salsa for dipping.

Makes 2 dozen wings

Prep and Cook Time: 55 minutes

Microwave Directions: Coat chicken as directed. Place 8 pieces on 9-inch microwaveable pie plate with meaty portions toward edge of plate. Microwave at MEDIUM-HIGH (70%) 8 to 10 minutes or until chicken is no longer pink near bone, turning dish after 4 minutes. (Chicken should reach an internal temperature of 180°F.) Repeat with remaining pieces. Serve as directed.

Dipper's Nuggets Chicken

2 boneless skinless chicken breasts,
  cut into 1-inch pieces (about
  1¼ pounds)
  Vegetable oil
1 egg
⅓ cup water
⅓ cup all-purpose flour
2 teaspoons sesame seed
1½ teaspoons salt
  Red onion rings for garnish
  Dipping Sauces (recipes follow)

Heat 3 inches oil in Dutch oven over medium-high heat until oil reaches 375°F. Meanwhile, beat egg and water in large bowl until combined. Add flour, sesame seed and salt; stir to form smooth batter. Dip chicken into batter, draining off excess. Fry chicken, a few pieces at a time, in hot oil about 4 minutes or until chicken is no longer pink in center. Drain on paper towels. Garnish with onion rings. Serve with Dipping Sauces. *Makes 8 servings*

Dipping Sauces

Nippy Pineapple Sauce: Mix 1 jar (12 ounces) pineapple preserves, ¼ cup prepared mustard and ¼ cup prepared horseradish in small saucepan. Cook and stir over low heat 5 minutes.

Dill Sauce: Combine ½ cup sour cream, ½ cup mayonnaise, 2 tablespoons finely chopped dill pickle and 1 teaspoon dried dill weed in small bowl. Cover and refrigerate 1 hour.

Royalty Sauce: Combine 1 cup catsup, 6 tablespoons butter or margarine, 2 tablespoons vinegar, 1 tablespoon brown sugar and ½ teaspoon dry mustard in small saucepan. Cook and stir over low heat 5 minutes.

*Favorite recipe from **National Broiler Council***

Dipper's Nuggets Chicken with Nippy Pineapple Sauce (top left), Royalty Sauce (top right) and Dill Sauce (bottom)

Mariachi Drumsticks

1¼ cups crushed plain tortilla chips
1 package (1.25 ounces) LAWRY'S®
   Taco Seasoning Mix
18 to 20 chicken drumettes
   Prepared salsa

Preheat oven to 350°F. In large plastic
bag, combine tortilla chips with Taco
Seasoning Mix. Dampen chicken with
water; shake off excess. Place chicken, a
few pieces at a time, in plastic bag; seal
and shake thoroughly to coat chicken
with chips. Arrange chicken in greased,
shallow baking pan; bake, uncovered,
30 minutes or until chicken is crispy.
Serve with salsa for dipping. Garnish
with parsley and lemon wedges, if
desired.   *Makes 18 to 20 drumettes*

Zesty Liver Pâté

⅓ cup butter or margarine
1 pound chicken livers
¾ cup coarsely chopped green onions
¾ cup chopped fresh parsley
½ cup dry white wine
¾ teaspoon TABASCO® Pepper Sauce
½ teaspoon salt
   Crackers or French bread

In large saucepan, melt butter; add
chicken livers, onions and parsley.
Sauté until livers are evenly browned
and cooked through. Transfer to
blender or food processor container.
Add wine, Tabasco® sauce and salt;
cover. Process until smooth. Pour into
decorative crock-style jar with lid. Chill
until thick enough to spread. Serve
with crackers.   *Makes about 2 cups pâté*

Thai Chicken Strips

½ cup WISH-BONE® Italian
   Dressing
¼ cup dry white wine
1 tablespoon sugar
1 tablespoon soy sauce
1 tablespoon finely chopped fresh
   cilantro or parsley
½ teaspoon ground ginger
½ teaspoon ground cumin
¼ teaspoon paprika
¼ cup sesame seed, toasted*
2 boneless skinless chicken breasts,
   cut lengthwise into strips
   (about 1¼ pounds)

In blender or food processor container,
process Italian Dressing, wine, sugar,
soy sauce, cilantro, ginger, cumin and
paprika until blended. In large, shallow
baking dish, combine dressing mixture,
sesame seed and chicken. Cover;
marinate in refrigerator, stirring
occasionally, at least 3 hours.

Remove chicken and marinade to large,
shallow baking pan or aluminum foil-
lined broiler rack. Broil chicken with
marinade, turning occasionally, 10
minutes or until chicken is no longer
pink in center. Garnish as desired.
    Makes about 20 chicken strips

•Also terrific with Wish-Bone® Robusto
Italian, Lite Italian, Blended Italian or
Lite Classic Dijon Vinaigrette Dressing.

*See page 20 for directions for toasting
sesame seed.

Mariachi Drumsticks

LUNCHEON FARE

These salads, sandwiches and soups make super midday meals. For the perfect light lunch, serve Calorie-Wise Dill Chicken or Chicken Avocado Boats.

Chicken Luncheon Sandwich

1½ cups chopped cooked chicken
1 cup (4 ounces) shredded
    Wisconsin Cheddar cheese
½ cup finely chopped celery
½ cup mayonnaise
½ cup plain yogurt
¼ cup green bell pepper
1 green onion, chopped
1 tablespoon chopped pimiento
    Salt and black pepper
    Bread or rolls
    Lettuce leaves

Combine chicken, cheese, celery, mayonnaise, yogurt, bell pepper, onion and pimiento. Season with salt and black pepper to taste. Stir until well blended. Refrigerate until ready to use. Serve on bread with lettuce.
    Makes about 4½ cups sandwich filling

Favorite recipe from **Wisconsin Milk Marketing Board** © *1992*

Cucumber Chicken Salad

3 tablespoons
    CROSSE & BLACKWELL®
    Worcestershire Sauce
2 tablespoons cider vinegar
2 tablespoons vegetable oil
1 tablespoon sesame oil
1 teaspoon sugar
1 teaspoon Dijon-style mustard
1 teaspoon grated fresh ginger
2 cups chopped cooked chicken
1 cup cooked spinach pasta (½ cup
    uncooked)
1 cucumber, peeled, seeded and
    sliced
1 red bell pepper, diced
¼ cup dry roasted peanuts

In large bowl, combine Worcestershire sauce, vinegar, vegetable oil, sesame oil, sugar, mustard and ginger. Add chicken, pasta, cucumber and red pepper; toss lightly to mix well. Top with peanuts.   *Makes 4 servings*

Chicken Luncheon Sandwich

Spinach Quiche

Preheat oven to 375°F. Cut leek in half lengthwise; wash and trim, leaving 2 to 3 inches of green tops intact. Cut leek halves crosswise into thin slices. Place in small saucepan; add enough water to cover. Bring to a boil over high heat; reduce heat and simmer 5 minutes. Drain; reserve leek.

Melt butter in large skillet over medium heat. Add chicken; cook until chicken is golden, about 5 minutes. Add spinach and leek to chicken mixture; cook 1 to 2 minutes longer. Remove from heat.

Spoon chicken mixture into pie crust. Sprinkle flour and cheese over chicken mixture. Combine eggs, half-and-half, brandy, salt, pepper and nutmeg in medium bowl. Pour egg mixture over cheese.

Bake 35 to 40 minutes or until knife inserted into center comes out clean. Let stand 5 minutes before serving. Serve hot or cold.　*Makes 6 servings*

Spinach Quiche

1 medium leek
　Water
¼ cup butter or margarine
2 cups finely chopped cooked
　chicken
½ package (10 ounces) frozen
　chopped spinach or broccoli,
　cooked and drained
1 unbaked ready-to-use pie crust
　(10 inches in diameter)
1 tablespoon all-purpose flour
1½ cups (6 ounces) shredded Swiss
　cheese
4 eggs
1½ cups half-and-half or evaporated
　milk
2 tablespoons brandy
½ teaspoon salt
¼ teaspoon pepper
¼ teaspoon ground nutmeg

Chicken Swiss-wiches

1½ cups chopped cooked chicken
⅓ cup mayonnaise
¼ cup diced celery
¼ cup diced Wisconsin Swiss cheese
8 slices bread
1 can (14½ ounces) asparagus
　spears, drained
½ cup butter
1 package (2⅜ ounces) seasoned
　coating mix for chicken

Combine chicken, mayonnaise, celery and cheese. Spread onto 4 bread slices. Arrange asparagus spears on top of filling; top with remaining bread slices.

Melt butter on griddle or in skillet; brush melted butter on outside of each sandwich. Dip each sandwich into coating mix. Grill until center is hot and coating is golden.　*Makes 4 servings*

*Favorite recipe from **Wisconsin Milk Marketing Board** © 1992*

Country Chicken Vegetable Soup

2 cans (13¾ ounces each) ready-to-serve chicken broth
½ teaspoon salt
½ teaspoon dried tarragon leaves
1 package (16 ounces) BIRDS EYE® Farm Fresh Mixtures, any variety
2 cups diced cooked chicken
½ cup MINUTE® Rice

Combine all ingredients, except rice, in large saucepan. Bring to a boil. Reduce heat; simmer 2 minutes. Stir in rice. Cover; remove from heat. Let stand 5 minutes. *Makes 6 servings*

Layered Chicken Salad

1 broiler-fryer chicken, cooked, skinned, boned, broken into pieces (about 2½ pounds)
1 can (8 ounces) water chestnuts, drained, sliced
2 cups alfalfa sprouts
1 small red onion, sliced into rings
½ cup oil-free Italian dressing
½ teaspoon freshly ground pepper

In medium glass bowl, layer half of chicken, water chestnuts, sprouts and onion rings. Sprinkle with half of dressing and pepper. Repeat layers; sprinkle with remaining dressing and pepper. Cover; refrigerate at least 2 hours. Serve cold. *Makes 4 servings*

*Favorite recipe from **National Broiler Council***

Country Chicken Vegetable Soup

Sweet and Spicy Chicken Salad

3 tablespoons peanut or
   vegetable oil
3 tablespoons rice vinegar
2 tablespoons soy sauce
1 tablespoon honey
1 teaspoon minced fresh ginger
1 teaspoon sesame oil
1 clove garlic, minced
1/4 teaspoon crushed red pepper
   flakes (optional)
4 cups chopped cooked chicken
4 cups packed shredded napa
   cabbage or romaine lettuce
1 cup shredded carrots
1/2 cup thinly sliced green onions
1 can (5 ounces) chow mein noodles
   (optional)
1/4 cup chopped cashews or peanuts
   (optional)
   Carrot curls and green onions for
   garnish

For dressing, combine peanut oil,
vinegar, soy sauce, honey, ginger,
sesame oil, garlic and crushed red
pepper in small jar with tight fitting
lid; shake well.

Place chicken in large bowl. Pour
dressing over chicken; toss to coat.* Add
cabbage, shredded carrots and sliced
onions to bowl; toss well to coat. Serve
over chow mein noodles. Sprinkle
cashews over salad. Garnish with carrot
curls and onions.

Makes 4 to 6 servings (about 8 cups salad)

*Salad may be made ahead to this
point; cover and refrigerate chicken
until ready to serve.

Grape Chef-Style Salad

Red Wine Vinaigrette (recipe
   follows)
1 1/2 cups California seedless grapes
5 ounces cubed cooked chicken
3 1/2 ounces Swiss cheese, cut into
   strips
1 cup sliced mushrooms
2 green onions, sliced diagonally
   into thin strips
4 cups torn lettuce

Prepare Red Wine Vinaigrette; set aside.
Combine grapes, chicken, cheese,
mushrooms and green onions in
medium bowl; pour vinaigrette over
mixture. Marinate, covered, in
refrigerator 1 hour. Drain; reserve
vinaigrette. Arrange lettuce in salad
bowl, leaving indentation in center.
Spoon marinated grape mixture into
center. Pass vinaigrette to serve over
greens.   *Makes 4 servings*

Red Wine Vinaigrette: Combine 1/3 cup
vegetable oil, 3 tablespoons red wine
vinegar, 1/2 teaspoon crushed oregano
leaves, 1/4 teaspoon salt, 1/8 teaspoon
ground black pepper and dash ground
red pepper in blender container or jar
with lid; blend well. Makes about
1/2 cup.

*Favorite recipe from **California Table Grape Commission***

Sweet and Spicy Chicken Salad

Lagoon Chicken Salad

2 whole chicken breasts
  (about 1½ pounds)
1½ cups unsweetened apple juice
3 cups cooked rice
1½ cups seedless green grapes, halved
1 cup chopped unpeeled apple
½ cup chopped celery
¾ cup slivered almonds, divided
½ cup chopped water chestnuts
1 cup mayonnaise
½ teaspoon seasoned salt
¼ teaspoon ground cinnamon
  Fresh spinach leaves
  Apple slices for garnish

Bring apple juice to a simmer in Dutch oven over medium heat; add chicken. Cover; simmer about 30 minutes or until chicken is no longer pink in center. Remove chicken; cool. Remove and discard skin and bones; dice chicken. Gently toss chicken with rice, grapes, chopped apple, celery, ½ cup almonds and water chestnuts in large bowl.

Combine mayonnaise, seasoned salt and cinnamon in small bowl; add to chicken-mayonnaise mixture and toss lightly. Cover; refrigerate at least 30 minutes. To serve, spoon chicken mixture onto spinach-lined platter. Sprinkle with remaining ¼ cup almonds; garnish with apple slices.

Makes 4 to 6 servings

*Favorite recipe from **National Broiler Council***

Lagoon Chicken Salad

Chicken Avocado Boats

Chicken Avocado Boats

   3 large ripe avocados, halved and
      pitted
   6 tablespoons lemon juice
   ¾ cup mayonnaise
  1½ tablespoons grated onion
   ¼ teaspoon celery salt
   ¼ teaspoon garlic powder
      Salt and pepper
   2 cups diced cooked chicken
   ½ cup (2 ounces) shredded sharp
      Cheddar cheese
      Snipped chives for garnish

Sprinkle each avocado half with
1 tablespoon lemon juice; set aside.

Preheat oven to 350°F. Combine
mayonnaise, onion, celery salt, garlic
powder and salt and pepper to taste in
medium bowl. Stir in chicken; mix well.

Drain any excess lemon juice from
avocado halves. Fill with chicken
mixture; sprinkle with cheese. Arrange
in single layer in baking dish. Pour
water into same dish to depth of
½ inch. Bake 15 minutes or until cheese
melts. Garnish with chives.

Makes 6 servings

Dijon Asparagus Chicken Salad

1 cup HELLMANN'S® or
   BEST FOODS® Real, Light or
   Cholesterol Free Reduced
   Calorie Mayonnaise
2 tablespoons Dijon-style mustard
2 tablespoons lemon juice
1 teaspoon salt
½ teaspoon freshly ground black
   pepper
6 ounces tricolor twist or spiral
   pasta, cooked, rinsed with cold
   water and drained
1 pound boneless skinless chicken
   breasts, cooked and cubed
1 package (10 ounces) frozen
   asparagus spears, thawed and
   cut into 2-inch pieces
1 red bell pepper, cut into 1-inch
   squares

In large bowl, combine mayonnaise,
mustard, lemon juice, salt and black
pepper. Stir in pasta, chicken,
asparagus and bell pepper. Cover; chill.

Makes 6 servings

Tropical Chicken Salad

Tropical Salad Dressing (recipe
   follows)
3 cups cubed cooked chicken
3/4 cup coarsely chopped celery
3/4 cup seedless red or green grape
   halves
3/4 cup coarsely chopped macadamia
   nuts or toasted almonds
Lettuce leaves
Strawberries and kiwifruit for
   garnish
Toasted flaked coconut for
   garnish*

Prepare Tropical Salad Dressing.
Combine chicken, celery, grapes and
nuts in large bowl; stir in *1 cup*
dressing. Cover; refrigerate 1 hour.
Mound chicken salad on lettuce-lined
platter or individual plates. Garnish
with strawberries, kiwifruit and
coconut. Serve with remaining dressing.
Makes 4 servings

Tropical Salad Dressing: Place 1/2 cup
COCO LOPEZ® Cream of Coconut, 1/3
cup red wine vinegar, 1 teaspoon dry
mustard, 1 teaspoon salt and 1 clove
garlic, peeled, in blender or food
processor container. With processor on,
slowly add 1 cup vegetable oil in thin
stream, processing until smooth.
(Refrigerate remaining dressing and
serve with fruit or mixed green salads.)

*To toast coconut, spread coconut in
shallow pan. Bake in preheated 350°F
oven 20 to 30 minutes or until lightly
browned, stirring occasionally.

Chunky Chicken Noodle Soup with Vegetables

2 envelopes LIPTON® Noodle Soup
   Mix with Real Chicken Broth
6 cups water
1/2 small head escarole, torn into
   pieces (about 2 cups) *or* 2 cups
   shredded cabbage
1 large rib celery, sliced
1 small carrot, sliced
1/4 cup frozen peas (optional)
1 small clove garlic, finely chopped
1/2 teaspoon dried thyme leaves
2 whole cloves
1 bay leaf
2 cups cubed cooked chicken
1 tablespoon finely chopped fresh
   parsley

Microwave Directions: In 3-quart
microwave-safe casserole, combine
noodle soup mix, water, escarole, celery,
carrot, peas, garlic, thyme, cloves and
bay leaf. Microwave, uncovered, at
HIGH, stirring occasionally, 20 minutes
or until vegetables are tender. Stir in
chicken and parsley; microwave,
uncovered, at HIGH 1 minute or until
heated through. Remove and discard
cloves and bay leaf. Let stand, covered,
5 minutes. *Makes about 4 servings*

Conventional Directions: In large
saucepan or stockpot, combine
ingredients as directed. Bring to a boil
over medium-high heat; reduce heat.
Simmer, uncovered, stirring
occasionally, 15 minutes or until
vegetables are tender. Stir in chicken
and parsley; heat through. Remove and
discard cloves and bay leaf.

Tropical Chicken Salad

Paella Salad

Garlic Dressing (recipe follows)
2½ cups water
1 cup uncooked rice
1 teaspoon salt
¼ to ½ teaspoon powdered saffron
2 cups cubed cooked chicken
1 cup cooked deveined medium
   shrimp (about 4 ounces)
1 cup diced cooked artichoke hearts
½ cup cooked peas
2 tablespoons chopped salami
2 tablespoons thinly sliced green
   onions
2 tablespoons chopped drained
   pimiento
1 tablespoon minced fresh parsley
Lettuce or fresh spinach leaves
1 large tomato, seeded and cubed

Prepare Garlic Dressing; set aside.

Bring water to a boil in 1-quart saucepan. Stir rice, salt and saffron into water. Reduce heat; cover and simmer 20 minutes. Remove from heat; let stand until water is absorbed, about 5 minutes. Refrigerate until cool, about 15 minutes.

Place cooled rice, chicken, shrimp, artichoke hearts, peas, salami, onions, pimiento and parsley in large bowl; toss well. Pour dressing over salad; toss lightly to coat. Cover; refrigerate 1 hour.

Arrange lettuce on large serving platter or individual serving plates; top with salad mixture. Garnish with tomato.

Makes 4 to 6 servings

Garlic Dressing

¾ cup olive or vegetable oil
¼ cup white wine vinegar
1 teaspoon salt
½ teaspoon pepper
1 clove garlic, pressed

Mix all ingredients in tightly covered jar. (Dressing can be refrigerated up to 2 weeks.)

Makes 1 cup

Garden Chicken Soup

2 cans (14½ ounces each)
   DEL MONTE® Italian Style
   Stewed Tomatoes
1 can (14½ ounces) low-salt chicken
   broth
½ pound boneless skinless chicken
   breasts or thighs, cut into strips
1 onion, chopped
1 rib celery, chopped
1 carrot, chopped
1 small potato, peeled and chopped
½ teaspoon dried thyme leaves,
   crushed

In large saucepan, combine all ingredients. Cover; simmer 20 minutes or until chicken is no longer pink in center and vegetables are tender.

Makes 4 to 6 servings

Prep and Cook Time: 30 minutes

Paella Salad

Chicken Cheese Burgers

3 cups ground chicken (12 to
   16 ounces)
2 eggs, slightly beaten
1 small onion, finely chopped
2 tablespoons plain dry bread
   crumbs, finely ground
2 tablespoons minced fresh parsley
1 tablespoon grated Parmesan cheese
1 teaspoon salt
¼ teaspoon baking soda
¼ teaspoon white pepper
¼ teaspoon dried oregano leaves
2 tablespoons butter or margarine
2 tablespoons vegetable oil
4 slices American or Cheddar cheese
   (1 ounce each)
4 large hamburger buns, separated
4 tablespoons mayonnaise
4 lettuce leaves
4 to 8 tomato slices

Chicken Cheese Burger

Combine chicken, eggs, onion, bread
crumbs, parsley, Parmesan cheese, salt,
baking soda, pepper and oregano in
large bowl; mix well. Shape chicken
mixture into 4 patties.

Heat butter and oil in large skillet over
medium-low heat until butter melts;
add patties. Cook until patties are no
longer pink in center, 4 to 5 minutes on
each side. Place 1 slice cheese on top of
each patty. Cover skillet; cook until
cheese melts, about 1 minute.

Spread each bun with 1 tablespoon
mayonnaise; arrange 1 lettuce leaf on
bottom half of each bun. Top with
chicken patty, tomato slices and top half
of bun. Serve hot.   *Makes 4 servings*

Chunky Chicken and Cucumber Salad

1 broiler-fryer chicken, cooked,
   skinned, boned, cut into chunks
   (about 2½ pounds)
2 cucumbers, peeled, cubed
1 red bell pepper, chopped
1 tablespoon apple cider vinegar
½ teaspoon salt
¼ teaspoon black pepper
¼ teaspoon seasoned salt
4 ounces plain nonfat yogurt
   Curly endive leaves

In medium bowl, mix cucumbers and
red pepper; sprinkle with vinegar, salt
and black pepper. Let stand about 5
minutes. Stir in chicken, seasoned salt
and yogurt, tossing gently. Cover; chill.
Serve on curly endive leaves.

Makes 4 servings

Favorite recipe from **National Broiler Council**

Soft Taco with Chicken

Stack tortillas; wrap in foil. Warm in 350°F oven 15 minutes or until heated through.

Melt butter in large skillet over medium heat. Add onion; cook until tender. Add chicken, green chilies and cilantro. Cook 3 minutes or until mixture is hot. Reduce heat to low. Stir in sour cream; season with salt and pepper to taste. Heat gently; *do not boil.*

To assemble each taco, spoon about 3 tablespoons chicken mixture into center of each tortilla; sprinkle with 2 tablespoons cheese. Top with equally divided amounts of avocado; drizzle with 1 to 2 teaspoons taco sauce. Sprinkle with remaining cheese. Roll tortilla into cone shape or fold in half and eat out of hand. Garnish as desired. *Makes 8 tacos*

Soft Tacos with Chicken

    8 corn tortillas (6 to 7 inches in
        diameter)
    2 tablespoons butter or margarine
    1 medium onion, chopped
1 1/2 cups shredded cooked chicken
    1 can (4 ounces) diced green chilies,
        drained
    2 tablespoons chopped fresh cilantro
    1 cup (1/2 pint) sour cream
        Salt and pepper
1 1/2 cups (6 ounces) shredded
        Monterey Jack cheese
    1 large avocado, halved, peeled,
        pitted and diced
        Prepared green taco sauce

Grecian Chicken Salad Sandwiches

    2 cups chopped cooked chicken
    1 cup seeded chopped cucumber
    1 cup seeded chopped tomato
  1/3 cup sliced green onions
  1/4 cup REALEMON® Lemon Juice
        from Concentrate
  1/4 cup vegetable oil
    1 teaspoon sugar
  1/2 teaspoon salt
  1/4 teaspoon dried basil leaves
    1 clove garlic, finely chopped
    2 cups shredded lettuce
    4 pita bread rounds, halved

In medium bowl, combine chicken, cucumber, tomato and green onions. In jar or cruet, combine ReaLemon® brand, oil, sugar, salt, basil and garlic; shake well. Pour over chicken mixture. Cover; marinate in refrigerator 2 hours. Just before serving, toss with lettuce. Serve in pita bread. Refrigerate leftovers.

Makes 4 servings

Fresh Fruity Chicken Salad

Fresh Fruity Chicken Salad

Yogurt Dressing (recipe follows)
2 cups cubed cooked chicken
1 cup cantaloupe balls
1 cup honeydew melon cubes
$^1/_2$ cup chopped celery
$^1/_3$ cup cashews
$^1/_4$ cup sliced green onions
Lettuce leaves

Prepare Yogurt Dressing; set aside. Combine chicken, melons, celery, cashews and onions in large bowl. Add dressing; mix lightly. Cover. Refrigerate 1 hour. Serve on bed of lettuce.

Makes 4 servings

Yogurt Dressing

$^1/_4$ cup plain yogurt
3 tablespoons mayonnaise
3 tablespoons fresh lime juice
$^3/_4$ teaspoon ground coriander
$^1/_2$ teaspoon salt
Dash of pepper

Combine ingredients in small bowl; mix well. *Makes about $^1/_2$ cup*

Italian Bean Soup

1 package (10 ounces) frozen Italian
    green beans
4 cups chicken broth
¹/₂ cup tomato sauce
¹/₂ teaspoon salt
¹/₄ teaspoon garlic salt
¹/₄ teaspoon dried oregano leaves
¹/₈ teaspoon dried dill weed
¹/₈ teaspoon pepper
¹/₃ cup uncooked soup macaroni
1 cup chopped cooked chicken

Place beans and next 7 ingredients in
2-quart saucepan. Bring to a boil over
high heat; stir in macaroni. Reduce heat
to low; cover and simmer 10 minutes.
Add chicken; cook 5 minutes.

Makes 4 to 6 servings

Cheesy Chicken
Sandwiches

¹/₄ cup chopped onion
2 tablespoons butter or margarine
2 tablespoons all-purpose flour
1¹/₂ cups milk
¹/₂ cup (2 ounces) shredded Swiss
    cheese
¹/₄ cup grated Parmesan cheese
¹/₂ teaspoon TABASCO® Pepper Sauce
    Pinch ground nutmeg
8 slices white bread, toasted
³/₄ pound sliced cooked chicken
8 slices cooked bacon, divided

Preheat broiler. In small saucepan, cook
onion in melted butter 3 minutes. Stir
in flour; cook 1 minute. Gradually stir
in milk. Bring to a boil over medium
heat and boil 1 minute; stir often. Add
cheeses, Tabasco® sauce and nutmeg;
stir until cheeses melt.

Place 4 slices toast in shallow baking
dish. Arrange chicken on toast; top
each sandwich with 1 slice bacon.
Spoon sauce over all. Broil until bubbly
and brown. Top with remaining bacon
and toast.

Makes 4 servings

Hot Chinese Chicken Salad

8 boneless skinless chicken thighs,
    cut into bite-size pieces
    (about 2 pounds)
¹/₄ cup cornstarch
¹/₄ cup vegetable oil
1 large ripe tomato, cut into wedges
1 can (4 ounces) water chestnuts,
    drained and sliced
1 can (4 ounces) sliced mushrooms,
    drained
1 cup coarsely chopped green onions
1 cup diagonally sliced celery
¹/₄ cup soy sauce
1 teaspoon monosodium glutamate
¹/₈ teaspoon garlic powder
2 cups shredded iceberg lettuce
    Orange slices for garnish
    Hot cooked rice

Dredge chicken, one piece at a time, in
cornstarch. Heat oil in wok or large
skillet over medium-high heat. Add
chicken; stir-fry about 3 minutes or
until browned and no longer pink in
center. Add tomato, water chestnuts,
mushrooms, green onions, celery, soy
sauce, monosodium glutamate and
garlic powder. Cover; simmer 5
minutes. Place lettuce on large serving
plate. Top with chicken mixture; garnish
with orange slices. Serve with rice.

Makes 4 servings

*Favorite recipe from **National Broiler Council***

Hot Chinese Chicken Salad

Montmorency Cherry Chicken Salad

New Yorker Pita Sandwich

**3/4 pound boneless skinless chicken
    breasts, cut into 1/4-inch strips**
1/2 cup chopped onion
1/2 cup green bell pepper strips
1 tablespoon vegetable oil
**1 can (16 ounces) HEINZ® Vegetarian
    Beans in Tomato Sauce**
**2 tablespoons HEINZ® Horseradish
    Sauce**
**1/4 teaspoon salt
    Dash black pepper**
**4 pocket pita breads (5 inches in
    diameter)**
**8 slices tomato
    Lettuce leaves**

In skillet, sauté chicken, onion and
green pepper in oil until vegetables are
tender-crisp and chicken is tender. Stir
in beans, horseradish sauce, salt and
black pepper. Simmer 5 minutes to
blend flavors. Cut pitas in half; tuck 1
tomato slice and some lettuce into each
half. Fill each with about 1/3 cup bean
mixture.

Makes 4 servings (about 3 cups mixture)

Montmorency Cherry Chicken Salad

3 nectarines or peaches, divided
3 cups cubed cooked chicken
**2 cups tart red Montmorency
    cherries, pitted***
1 1/2 cups sliced celery
2 tablespoons sliced green onions
1 cup mayonnaise
1/4 cup sour cream
2 tablespoons honey
1 teaspoon lemon juice
1/4 to 1/2 teaspoon curry powder
**1/8 teaspoon ground ginger
    Salt**
**1/2 cup toasted slivered almonds,
    divided****
    Boston or Bibb lettuce leaves**

Slice 1 nectarine; combine with chicken,
cherries, celery and onions in large
bowl. Combine mayonnaise, sour
cream, honey, lemon juice, curry
powder and ginger in small bowl,
mixing well. Season with salt to taste.
Pour mayonnaise mixture over chicken
mixture; toss to coat. Cover; refrigerate
1 hour. Just before serving, stir in all
but 1 tablespoon almonds. Arrange
chicken salad on lettuce-lined salad
plates. Slice remaining 2 nectarines;
garnish individual salads with
nectarines and remaining 1 tablespoon
almonds.   *Makes 6 servings*

*Fresh, canned or frozen cherries may
be used. Thaw frozen cherries. Drain
canned and thawed cherries before
using.

**To toast almonds, spread almonds in
shallow pan. Bake in preheated 350°F
oven 8 to 10 minutes or until golden
brown, stirring frequently.

*Favorite recipe from **New York Cherry Growers
Association***

Mexican-Style Almond Chicken Salad

1 cup BLUE DIAMOND® Blanched
   Slivered Almonds
   Vegetable oil
6 tablespoons lime juice
3 cloves garlic, finely chopped
5 teaspoons ground cumin
1/2 teaspoon salt
1/8 teaspoon ground red pepper
6 tablespoons mayonnaise
2 boneless skinless chicken breasts,
   halved, poached and cut into
   1-inch cubes (about 1 1/4 pounds)
1 small red onion, chopped
2 oranges, peeled, diced
4 flour tortillas (7 to 8 inches in
   diameter)
   Lettuce leaves
   Sliced avocado, peeled orange
   slices, red onion rings and
   BLUE DIAMOND® Blanched
   Slivered Almonds for garnish

In small skillet over medium heat, sauté
1 cup almonds in 2 teaspoons oil until
golden; reserve. Combine lime juice,
garlic, cumin, salt and ground red
pepper in large bowl. Beat in
mayonnaise and 1/3 cup oil. Add
chicken, onion and almonds. Gently
fold in diced oranges. Heat 2 inches oil
in Dutch oven. Fry tortillas in oil, one at
a time, turning once, until crisp, puffed
and golden; drain and reserve. (A metal
ladle can be pressed in center of tortilla
while frying to form shell.) To serve,
line each fried tortilla with lettuce
leaves; top with 1/4 of chicken salad.
Garnish each serving with avocado
slices, orange slices and onion rings.
Top each serving with almonds.

Makes 4 servings

Tomato, Chicken and Mushroom Soup

1/4 pound mushrooms, sliced*
1 tablespoon butter or margarine
2 cans (13 3/4 ounces each) ready-to-
   serve chicken broth
2 cups diced cooked chicken
1 can (14 1/2 ounces) whole tomatoes
1 can (8 ounces) tomato sauce
1 carrot, thinly sliced
1 envelope GOOD SEASONS®
   Italian Salad Dressing Mix
3/4 cup MINUTE® Rice

Cook and stir mushrooms in hot butter
in large saucepan. Gradually stir in
broth; add chicken, tomatoes, tomato
sauce, carrot and salad dressing mix.
Bring to a boil; reduce heat. Cover;
simmer 10 minutes. Stir in rice. Cover;
remove from heat. Let stand 5 minutes.

Makes 8 servings

*Substitute 1 jar (4.5 ounces) drained,
sliced mushrooms for the fresh
mushrooms.

Tomato, Chicken and Mushroom Soup

Calorie-Wise Dill Chicken

12 chicken drumsticks (about
   2 pounds)
1 cup plain low-fat yogurt
1½ cups natural wheat germ
½ cup chopped almonds
2 teaspoons dried dill weed
½ teaspoon salt
¼ teaspoon pepper
   Nonstick vegetable cooking spray

Preheat oven to 350°F. Place yogurt in
shallow bowl. Combine wheat germ,
almonds, dill, salt and pepper in
another shallow bowl. Dip drumsticks,
one at a time, into yogurt; roll each in
wheat germ mixture to coat. Line
baking sheet with aluminum foil; spray
with nonstick vegetable cooking spray.
Arrange chicken in single layer on foil.
Bake about 50 minutes or until chicken
is tender and juices run clear. Garnish
as desired. *Makes 4 servings*

Favorite recipe from **National Broiler Council**

Chinese Chicken Salad

½ cup mayonnaise
2 tablespoons
   CROSSE & BLACKWELL®
   Worcestershire Sauce
1 tablespoon dry sherry
1 teaspoon sugar
1½ cups cubed cooked chicken
1 can (8 ounces) sliced water
   chestnuts, drained
1 cup red seedless grapes
1 can (8 ounces) pineapple chunks,
   drained
2 carrots, peeled, shredded
3 green onions, sliced

In large bowl, combine mayonnaise,
Worcestershire sauce, sherry and sugar.
Add chicken, water chestnuts, grapes,
pineapple, carrots and green onions;
stir to coat with dressing. Cover;
refrigerate 30 minutes.
Makes 4 servings

Calorie-Wise Dill Chicken

Fandangled Fajitas Salad

**1 pound boneless skinless chicken
   breasts, thinly sliced**
1 tablespoon vegetable oil
**1 package (1.27 ounces) LAWRY'S®
   Spices & Seasonings for Fajitas**
¼ cup water
4 cups shredded lettuce
**1 can (15 ounces) pinto beans,
   drained and rinsed**
1 medium onion, slivered
**1 medium green or red bell pepper,
   slivered**
1 medium tomato, thinly sliced
**1 avocado, halved, peeled, pitted
   and thinly sliced**
**Fandangled Dressing (recipe
   follows)**

In large skillet, brown chicken pieces in
hot oil; drain fat. Add Spices &
Seasonings for Fajitas and water; blend
well. Bring to a boil; reduce heat and
simmer, uncovered, 3 to 5 minutes. On
individual serving plates, arrange
lettuce; layer beans, onion, green
pepper, tomato and avocado. Top with
equal portions of prepared fajitas
mixture. Serve Fandangled Dressing on
the side.   *Makes 4 servings*

Fandangled Dressing

1⅓ cups chunky prepared salsa
¼ cup vegetable oil
2 tablespoons red wine vinegar
2 tablespoons lime juice

In container with stopper or lid,
combine all ingredients; blend well.
                Makes about 1½ cups

Presentation: Serve with tortilla chips.

Calico Chicken Soup

Calico Chicken Soup

**1 pound skinned boneless chicken
   breasts, cut into chunks**
1 tablespoon vegetable oil
6 cups water
**2 tablespoons WYLER'S® or
   STEERO® Chicken-Flavor Instant
   Bouillon *or* 6 Chicken-Flavor
   Bouillon Cubes**
2 cups broccoli flowerets
2 cups sliced pared carrots
¾ cup chopped red bell pepper
¼ teaspoon black pepper

In large kettle or Dutch oven, brown
chicken in oil. Add remaining
ingredients. Bring to a boil; reduce heat.
Simmer, uncovered, 45 minutes, stirring
occasionally. Refrigerate leftovers.
                Makes about 2 quarts soup

Arroz con Pollo Burritos
Chicken with Rice Burritos

2½ cups shredded cooked chicken
1 package (1.25 ounces) LAWRY'S®
    Taco Spices & Seasonings
3¼ cups water
1 cup long-grain rice
2 tablespoons vegetable oil
1 can (8 ounces) tomato sauce
1 teaspoon LAWRY'S® Lemon
    Pepper Seasoning
1 large tomato, chopped
¼ cup chopped green onions
8 medium flour tortillas, warmed
    Grated Cheddar cheese

In large, deep skillet, combine chicken, Taco Spices & Seasonings and ³/₄ cup water. Bring to a boil; reduce heat. Simmer, uncovered, 10 minutes. Remove chicken mixture; set aside. In same skillet, sauté rice in hot oil until golden. Add remaining 2½ cups water, tomato sauce and Lemon Pepper Seasoning. Bring to a boil; reduce heat. Cover; simmer 20 minutes. Stir in chicken mixture, tomato and onions; blend well. Heat 5 minutes. Place heaping ½ cup filling on each tortilla. Fold in sides; roll to enclose filling. Place filled burritos, seam side down, on baking sheet. Sprinkle with cheese. Heat in 350°F oven 5 minutes to melt cheese. *Makes 8 servings*

Presentation: Garnish with salsa and guacamole.

Cherry Chicken Salad

1 can (16 ounces) pitted tart cherries,
    undrained (about 1½ cups)
4 small boneless skinless chicken
    breasts (about 1 pound)
3 cups cooked wild rice
1 cup chopped apple
³/₄ cup chopped walnuts
½ cup chopped celery
½ cup golden raisins
    Cherry Dressing (recipe follows)
    Lettuce leaves

Drain cherries, reserving ½ cup cherry juice for Cherry Dressing and ¼ cup cherries for garnish. Add water to remaining cherry juice to make 1½ cups; place in large saucepan with chicken. Cook chicken over medium heat 15 minutes or until no longer pink in center. Meanwhile, prepare Cherry Dressing.

Remove chicken from saucepan; cut into small pieces. Combine chicken, remaining cherries, rice, apple, walnuts, celery and raisins in large bowl; cover and refrigerate 1 hour. Add Cherry Dressing; mix well. Serve on lettuce-lined platter; garnish with ¼ cup reserved cherries.

Makes 8 to 10 servings

Cherry Dressing

½ cup reserved cherry juice
½ cup vegetable oil
½ cup grated Parmesan cheese
3 tablespoons sugar
⅛ teaspoon garlic powder
⅛ teaspoon pepper
⅛ teaspoon dried basil leaves
⅛ teaspoon dried oregano leaves

Combine all ingredients.

Favorite recipe from New York Cherry Growers Association

Arroz con Pollo Burritos

Rainbow Chicken Salad

Rainbow Chicken Salad

2 whole chicken breasts (about
   1¹/₂ pounds)
2 cups water
1 teaspoon salt
¹/₄ teaspoon pepper
   Orange-Mustard Mayonnaise
   (recipe follows)
1 head romaine lettuce
2 avocados, halved, peeled, pitted
   and sliced lengthwise
2 grapefruit, peeled and sectioned
   Juice of 1 lemon
4 navel oranges, peeled and
   sectioned
1 red onion, sliced into rings
   Orange zest for garnish*

Bring water to a simmer in Dutch oven over medium heat; add chicken, salt and pepper. Cover; simmer about 30 minutes or until chicken is no longer pink in center. While chicken is cooking, prepare Orange-Mustard Mayonnaise. Remove chicken from Dutch oven; cool. (Reserve broth for another use, if desired.) Remove and discard skin and bones; cut chicken into thin slices. Set aside.

Arrange lettuce leaves on large platter with stems toward center. Alternately arrange avocado slices and grapefruit sections around edges of lettuce; sprinkle with lemon juice. Arrange orange sections and onion rings inside avocados and grapefruit. Arrange chicken in center. Spoon some Orange-Mustard Mayonnaise over chicken; garnish with orange zest. Serve with remaining mayonnaise.

Makes 4 to 6 servings

Orange-Mustard Mayonnaise: Beat 2 egg yolks** with 2 teaspoons Dijon-style mustard and 1 teaspoon lemon juice in medium bowl. Gradually add 1 cup olive oil, a few drops at a time, beating with wire whisk until 3 tablespoons have been added. Then, pour in remaining olive oil in a thin, steady stream, beating constantly, until mixture thickens. Stir in grated peel of 1 orange, juice from ¹/₂ orange and salt and pepper to taste.

*The colored outer portion of citrus peel is called *zest*. To remove zest, use a vegetable peeler, zester or grater, taking care to remove only the zest and *not* the white *pith* underneath, which is bitter.

**Use clean, uncracked eggs.

*Favorite recipe from **National Broiler Council***

Chicken Cilantro Bisque

6 ounces boneless skinless chicken
   breasts, cut into chunks
2½ cups low-sodium chicken broth
½ cup fresh cilantro leaves
½ cup sliced green onions
¼ cup sliced celery
1 large clove garlic, minced
½ teaspoon ground cumin
⅓ cup all-purpose flour
1½ cups (12-ounce can) *undiluted*
   CARNATION® Evaporated
   Skimmed Milk
   Fresh ground pepper

In large saucepan, combine chicken,
broth, cilantro, green onions, celery,
garlic and cumin. Heat to boiling;
reduce heat and simmer gently,
covered, 15 minutes. Pour soup into
blender or food processor container.
Add flour. Cover and blend at low
speed until smooth. Pour mixture back
into saucepan. Cook over medium heat,
stirring constantly, until mixture comes
to a boil and thickens. Remove from
heat. Gradually stir in milk. Reheat just
to serving temperature. *Do not boil.*
Season with pepper to taste. Garnish as
desired.   *Makes about 4 servings*

Chicken Cilantro Bisque

Sizzling Chicken Sandwich

Sizzling Chicken Sandwiches

2 boneless skinless chicken breasts,
   halved (about 1¼ pounds)
1 package (1.27 ounces) LAWRY'S®
   Spices & Seasonings for Fajitas
1 cup chunky prepared salsa
¼ cup water
   Lettuce
4 large sandwich buns
4 slices Monterey Jack cheese
   Red onion slices
   Avocado slices
   Chunky prepared salsa

Place chicken in large, resealable plastic
bag. In small bowl, combine Spices &
Seasonings for Fajitas, 1 cup salsa and
water; pour over chicken. Marinate in
refrigerator 2 hours. Remove chicken;
reserve marinade. Grill or broil chicken
5 to 7 minutes on each side, basting
frequently with marinade, until chicken
is tender and juices run clear.* Place on
lettuce-lined sandwich buns. Top with
cheese, onion, avocado and salsa.
   Makes 4 servings

*Do not baste chicken with marinade
during last 5 minutes of cooking.

Lipton® Fried Rice with Chicken

2 tablespoons vegetable oil, divided
1 cup chopped bok choy (Chinese cabbage) or green cabbage
1 cup snow peas
1/4 cup sliced green onions
1 clove garlic, finely chopped
1 pound boneless skinless chicken breasts, cut into thin strips
1 envelope LIPTON® Onion-Mushroom Recipe Soup Mix
3/4 cup water
1 tablespoon soy sauce
1/8 teaspoon pepper
2 cups cooked brown or white rice (cooked in unsalted water)

Heat 1 tablespoon oil in wok or large skillet over medium-high heat. Add bok choy, snow peas, green onions and garlic; stir-fry 3 minutes or until vegetables are crisp-tender. Remove vegetables; reserve. Heat remaining 1 tablespoon oil in wok. Add chicken strips; stir-fry 3 minutes or until tender. Thoroughly blend soup mix, water, soy sauce and pepper in small bowl; stir into chicken in wok. Add cooked rice and reserved vegetables; heat through and serve.   *Makes about 4 servings*

Lipton® Fried Rice with Chicken

Chicken and Vegetables on Toast Points

2 boneless skinless chicken breasts, cut into 1-inch pieces (about 1 1/4 pounds)
1 tablespoon butter-flavored margarine
1/2 teaspoon salt
1/4 teaspoon pepper
1 1/2 cups sour cream
1 teaspoon soy sauce
1 teaspoon paprika
2 tablespoons white wine
1 package (5 ounces) frozen peas, pearl onions and mushrooms, cooked according to package directions
1/4 cup (1 ounce) freshly grated Parmesan cheese
6 slices bread, toasted, cut into 4 triangles

In 10-inch nonstick skillet, melt margarine over medium heat. Arrange chicken in single layer in skillet; cook about 4 minutes. Turn; cook chicken until light brown, about 4 minutes more. Sprinkle with salt and pepper. Stir in sour cream, soy sauce and paprika. Reduce heat to low; cook until heated through, about 4 minutes. Stir in white wine; cook 1 minute. Add hot cooked peas, pearl onions and mushrooms. Pour mixture into greased, 1 1/2-quart shallow broiler-proof baking dish. Sprinkle with cheese; broil in oven until light brown, about 4 minutes. Serve mixture over toast points.
Makes 6 servings

Favorite recipe from National Broiler Council

Chicken Potato Salad Olé

Chicken Potato Salad Olé

2 large ripe tomatoes, seeded and
    chopped
³/₄ cup chopped green onions
¹/₄ cup fresh cilantro leaves, chopped
1 to 2 tablespoons chopped, seeded,
    pickled jalapeño peppers
1¹/₂ teaspoons salt, divided
1 cup HELLMANN'S® or
    BEST FOODS® Real, Light or
    Cholesterol Free Reduced
    Calorie Mayonnaise
3 tablespoons lime juice
1 teaspoon chili powder
1 teaspoon ground cumin
2 pounds small red potatoes, cooked
    and sliced ¹/₄ inch thick
2 cups shredded cooked chicken
1 large yellow or red bell pepper,
    diced
  Lettuce leaves
  Tortilla chips, lime slices, whole
    chili peppers and cilantro sprigs
    for garnish (optional)

In medium bowl, combine tomatoes,
onions, chopped cilantro, jalapeño
peppers and 1 teaspoon salt; set aside.
In large bowl, combine mayonnaise,
lime juice, chili powder, cumin and
remaining ¹/₂ teaspoon salt. Add
potatoes, chicken, bell pepper and half
of tomato mixture; toss to coat well.
Cover; chill. To serve, spoon salad onto
lettuce-lined platter. Spoon remaining
tomato mixture over salad. If desired,
garnish with tortilla chips, lime slices,
whole chili peppers and cilantro sprigs.
Makes 6 servings

Larry's Pineapple Hula Salad

2 cans (8 ounces each) DOLE®
    Pineapple Chunks, drained
2 cups cubed cooked chicken
1 cup diagonally sliced celery
1 cup diced papaya
1/2 cup macadamia nuts or peanuts
1 cup mayonnaise
2 teaspoons curry powder
    Crisp salad greens
    Chives and sliced kumquats for
    garnish

Combine pineapple, chicken, celery, papaya and nuts in large bowl. Blend mayonnaise and curry powder in small bowl; pour over chicken mixture. Blend thoroughly. Cover; chill at least 1 hour. Serve mounded on salad greens. Garnish with chives and kumquats.

Makes 4 servings

Chicken Corn Chowder

4 slices bacon
1/2 cup chopped onion
1/2 teaspoon thyme leaves
3 tablespoons unsifted flour
3 cups BORDEN® or MEADOW GOLD®
    Half-and-Half *or* Milk
2 cups water
1 1/2 cups cubed cooked chicken
1 (10-ounce) package frozen whole
    kernel corn
1 medium potato, pared and diced
2 tablespoons WYLER'S® or
    STEERO® Chicken-Flavor Instant
    Bouillon *or* 6 Chicken-Flavor
    Bouillon Cubes
1/4 teaspoon pepper

In large saucepan, cook bacon until crisp; remove and crumble. In drippings, cook onion and thyme until tender; stir in flour until blended. Add remaining ingredients except bacon; bring to a boil. Reduce heat; simmer 30 minutes or until vegetables are tender, stirring occasionally. Garnish with bacon. Refrigerate leftovers.

Makes about 1 3/4 quarts chowder

Tip: Two 5- or 6 3/4-ounce cans chunk chicken can be substituted for cooked chicken; add during last 10 minutes of cooking time.

Confetti Chicken Salad

1/4 cup white vinegar
3 tablespoons Chef Paul
    Prudhomme's
    POULTRY MAGIC®
1 teaspoon ground allspice
1/2 teaspoon crumbled bay leaf*
1/2 teaspoon salt
1 cup vegetable oil
4 cups cooked rice
12 ounces cooked chicken, cut into
    bite-size pieces
2 cups small broccoli florets
2 cups chopped fresh tomatoes
1 cup shredded carrots
1/2 cup chopped onion
1/2 cup chopped celery
    Lettuce leaves

Combine vinegar, Poultry Magic®, allspice, bay leaf and salt in blender or food processor container. Process until well mixed and bay leaf is finely ground. With motor running, add oil in slow, steady stream until dressing is thick and creamy. Combine remaining ingredients except lettuce in large mixing bowl. Stir in dressing. Line 6 serving plates with lettuce. Mound even portions of chicken salad over lettuce.

Makes 6 servings

*Remove stems and crumble by hand.

Larry's Pineapple Hula Salad

Hearty Chicken and Rice Soup

10 cups chicken broth
1 medium onion, chopped
1 cup sliced celery
1 cup sliced carrots
1/4 cup snipped fresh parsley
1/2 teaspoon cracked black pepper
1/2 teaspoon dried thyme leaves
1 bay leaf
3/4 pound boneless skinless chicken, cubed
2 cups cooked rice
2 tablespoons lime juice
Lime slices for garnish

Combine broth, onion, celery, carrots, parsley, pepper, thyme, and bay leaf in Dutch oven. Bring to a boil; stir once or twice. Reduce heat; simmer, uncovered, 10 to 15 minutes. Add chicken; simmer, uncovered, 5 to 10 minutes or until chicken is cooked. Remove and discard bay leaf. Stir in rice and lime juice just before serving. Garnish with lime slices.

Makes about 8 servings

Favorite recipe from **USA Rice Council**

Hearty Chicken and Rice Soup

Sesame Chicken Pita Pockets

1/4 cup reduced-calorie mayonnaise
1 tablespoon sesame or vegetable oil
1/4 teaspoon LAWRY'S® Garlic Powder with Parsley
3/4 pound boneless skinless chicken breasts, cut into thin strips
1 tablespoon soy sauce
3/4 teaspoon ground ginger
1 package (6 ounces) frozen Chinese pea pods, thawed
2 tablespoons margarine or butter, divided
1/2 teaspoon LAWRY'S® Seasoned Pepper
2 whole wheat pita breads, warmed
Lettuce leaves

In small bowl, combine mayonnaise, oil and Garlic Powder with Parsley; blend well. Chill.

Sprinkle chicken pieces with soy sauce and ginger. In medium skillet, sauté pea pods in 1 tablespoon hot margarine 1 minute. Remove; set aside. In same skillet, sauté chicken in remaining 1 tablespoon hot margarine 5 to 7 minutes or until chicken is browned and juices run clear. Sprinkle with Seasoned Pepper.

Cut pita breads in half. Spread insides of pitas generously with mayonnaise mixture. Fill each with lettuce leaf, chicken and pea pods. Serve warm.

Makes 4 servings

Presentation: Arrange on platter and serve with fresh fruit.

Hint: For extra crunch, add sliced water chestnuts, cashews or peanuts to chicken mixture.

Fresh Apricot Thai Salad

Fresh Apricot Thai Salad

2 cups sliced fresh California
   apricots
2 cups cubed cooked chicken
1 cup sliced peeled cucumber
1 cup bean sprouts, rinsed
$^1/_4$ cup rice vinegar
1 tablespoon chopped fresh cilantro
2 teaspoons sugar
$^1/_4$ cup vegetable oil
$^1/_2$ teaspoon chili oil
   Lettuce leaves
2 tablespoons coarsely chopped
   peanuts

In large bowl, combine apricots, chicken, cucumber and sprouts; refrigerate. In small bowl, beat vinegar, cilantro and sugar until smooth. Drizzle in oils while vigorously whipping with wire whisk. Toss chilled salad with dressing; arrange on individual lettuce-lined plates. Sprinkle with peanuts.

Makes 4 servings

Favorite recipe from **California Apricot Advisory Board**

SUPPER TIME

For old-fashioned goodness, rely on these family favorites. Cornbread Chicken Pie and Magically Moist Chicken will send them back for seconds.

One-Skillet Spicy Chicken 'n Rice

¹/₄ cup all-purpose flour
1 teaspoon LAWRY'S® Seasoned Salt
6 to 8 chicken pieces, skinned
2 tablespoons vegetable oil
2 cans (14¹/₂ ounces each) whole peeled tomatoes, undrained and cut up
1 package (1.25 ounces) LAWRY'S® Taco Spices & Seasonings
1 cup thinly sliced celery
1 cup long-grain rice
¹/₂ cup chopped onion
Chopped fresh parsley

In plastic bag, combine flour and Seasoned Salt. Add chicken; shake to coat well. In large skillet over medium-high heat, brown chicken in hot oil; reduce heat to low. Cook, uncovered, 15 minutes. Add remaining ingredients except parsley; blend well. Bring to a boil; reduce heat. Cover; simmer 20 minutes or until liquid is absorbed and chicken is tender. Garnish with parsley.
Makes 4 to 6 servings

Chicken with Zesty Tuna Sauce

1 can (6¹/₂ ounces) tuna, drained
¹/₂ cup HELLMANN'S® or BEST FOODS® Real, Light or Cholesterol Free Reduced Calorie Mayonnaise
¹/₃ cup milk
1 tablespoon capers, rinsed and drained
2 anchovy fillets
2 tablespoons lemon juice
1 pound boneless skinless chicken breasts, cooked and sliced
3 tomatoes, sliced
1 tablespoon chopped fresh parsley

In blender or food processor container, place tuna, mayonnaise, milk, capers and anchovies. Process until smooth. Add lemon juice; process until blended. On large serving platter, alternately arrange chicken and tomato slices, overlapping slightly to form circle. Top with tuna sauce. Sprinkle with parsley.
Makes 4 servings

One-Skillet Spicy Chicken 'n Rice

Rick's Good-As-Gold Chili

Combine water, onion and garlic in small bowl; let stand 10 minutes to soften. Heat oil in large skillet over medium heat until hot. Add chicken, a few pieces at a time; cook until golden brown, about 5 minutes on each side. Remove and drain on paper towels. Cool slightly; cut into ¼-inch cubes and set aside.

Pour off all but 2 tablespoons oil from skillet; heat oil until hot. Add softened onion and garlic; cook and stir about 5 minutes or until golden. Add remaining ingredients and chicken; mix well. Bring to a boil; reduce heat and simmer about 20 minutes, stirring occasionally, until chili thickens slightly. Garnish as desired. *Makes 4½ cups chili*

*Favorite recipe from **American Spice Trade Association***

Rick's Good-As-Gold Chili

⅓ cup water
¼ cup instant minced onion
2 teaspoons instant minced garlic
½ cup vegetable oil
2 boneless skinless chicken breasts, cut into small pieces (about 1¼ pounds)
1 can (15 ounces) tomato sauce
¾ cup beer
½ cup chicken broth
2 tablespoons chili powder
2 teaspoons ground cumin
1 teaspoon dried oregano leaves, crushed
1 teaspoon soy sauce
1 teaspoon Worcestershire sauce
¾ teaspoon salt
½ teaspoon paprika
½ teaspoon ground red pepper
¼ teaspoon ground turmeric
⅛ teaspoon rubbed sage
⅛ teaspoon dried thyme leaves, crushed
⅛ teaspoon dry mustard

Gypsy Chicken

6 chicken thighs (about 2 pounds)
2 teaspoons vegetable oil
1 can (14½ ounces) DEL MONTE® Italian Style Stewed Tomatoes
2 cups sliced mushrooms
¼ teaspoon dried thyme leaves, crushed
¼ teaspoon ground sage
1 cup (4 ounces) shredded Monterey Jack cheese

In skillet, cook chicken on both sides in oil over medium-high heat until chicken is browned and juices run clear, about 15 minutes; drain. Remove chicken; keep warm. In same skillet, cook tomatoes, mushrooms and seasonings over medium-high heat 5 minutes or until thickened, stirring frequently. Add chicken and cheese; cook until heated through and cheese melts.

Makes 4 servings

Prep and Cook Time: 28 minutes

Bittersweet Farm Chicken

1 broiler-fryer chicken, cut up
    (3$\frac{1}{2}$ to 4 pounds)
$\frac{1}{2}$ cup all-purpose flour
1 teaspoon salt
$\frac{1}{4}$ teaspoon pepper
8 tablespoons butter or margarine,
    divided
$\frac{1}{4}$ cup lemon juice
$\frac{1}{4}$ cup orange-flavored liqueur
$\frac{1}{4}$ cup honey
2 tablespoons orange zest*
1 tablespoon soy sauce
    Whole cooked baby carrots

Preheat oven to 350°F. Combine flour, salt and pepper in large plastic bag. Add chicken pieces, a few at a time; shake to coat completely with flour mixture. Melt 4 tablespoons butter in large baking pan. Roll chicken in butter to coat all sides; arrange, skin side down, in single layer in pan. Bake 30 minutes.

Meanwhile, melt remaining 4 tablespoons butter in small saucepan over medium heat. Stir in lemon juice, liqueur, honey, orange zest and soy sauce; reserve 2 tablespoons mixture. Remove chicken from oven; turn pieces over. Pour remaining honey mixture over chicken. Continue baking, basting occasionally, 30 minutes or until chicken is glazed and fork can be inserted into chicken with ease. Toss reserved 2 tablespoons honey mixture with cooked carrots; serve with chicken. Garnish as desired.   *Makes 4 servings*

*See page 48 for information about zest.

*Favorite recipe from **National Broiler Council***

Bittersweet Farm Chicken

Orange Chicken Oriental

1 can (8¼ ounces) pineapple
  chunks, undrained
3 boneless skinless chicken breasts,
  cut into 2-inch pieces (about
  2 pounds)
½ teaspoon salt
¼ teaspoon ground ginger
2 tablespoons vegetable oil
1 small clove garlic, minced
1 cup Florida orange juice, divided
1 teaspoon instant chicken-flavored
  bouillon granules
2 tablespoons white wine vinegar
⅓ cup sliced celery
1 small green bell pepper, cut into
  ¼-inch strips
1 small onion, sliced
1 small tomato, cut into wedges
3 tablespoons all-purpose flour
2 tablespoons soy sauce
1 tablespoon sugar
  Hot cooked rice

Drain pineapple, reserving juice; set
aside. Sprinkle chicken with salt and
ginger. Heat oil in large skillet over
medium heat. Add chicken and garlic;
cook 5 minutes. Add reserved pineapple
juice, ¾ cup orange juice, bouillon and
vinegar. Cover; simmer 10 minutes or
until chicken is tender and juices run
clear.

Add celery, green pepper and onion.
Cover; cook 5 minutes. Add tomato and
pineapple. In small bowl, blend
together flour, soy sauce, sugar and
remaining ¼ cup orange juice. Add to
skillet and cook, stirring constantly,
until mixture thickens and comes to a
boil; cook 1 minute. Serve over rice.

Makes 4 servings

*Favorite recipe from **Florida Department of Citrus***

Jiffy Chicken 'n Rice

1½ cups hot cooked unsalted rice
  (½ cup uncooked)
1 jar (8 ounces) pasteurized process
  cheese food
¼ cup milk
2 cups (10 ounces) cubed cooked
  chicken
1 package (10 ounces) frozen peas,
  thawed and drained
1 can (2.8 ounces) DURKEE® French
  Fried Onions

Preheat oven to 375°F. To rice in
saucepan, add cheese food, milk,
chicken, peas and *½ can* French Fried
Onions; stir well. Spoon into 1½-quart
casserole. Bake, uncovered, 25 minutes
or until heated through. Top with
remaining onions; bake, uncovered, 3
minutes or until onions are golden
brown.   *Makes 4 to 6 servings*

Microwave Directions: Prepare rice
mixture as directed; spoon into 1½-
quart microwave-safe casserole.
Microwave, covered, on HIGH 8 to 10
minutes or until heated through. Stir
rice mixture halfway through cooking
time. Top with remaining onions;
microwave, uncovered, on HIGH 1
minute. Let stand 5 minutes before
serving.

Orange Chicken Oriental

Chicken Smothered with Black-Eyed Peas

1 tablespoon salt
2½ teaspoons onion powder, divided
4½ teaspoons garlic powder, divided
1 teaspoon white pepper
1 teaspoon dry mustard
2½ teaspoons rubbed sage, divided
1½ teaspoons dried thyme leaves, divided
1 stewing or roasting chicken, cut up (3½ to 4 pounds)
1 cup all-purpose flour
Vegetable oil
9 slices bacon, cut into ½-inch pieces
3 medium onions, finely chopped
1½ cups finely chopped celery
3 bay leaves
1 tablespoon plus 1 teaspoon TABASCO® Pepper Sauce, divided
1 pound dried black-eyed peas
11 cups chicken stock or water
Hot cooked rice

In small bowl, combine salt, 1½ teaspoons onion powder, 1½ teaspoons garlic powder, white pepper, mustard, 1 teaspoon sage and ½ teaspoon thyme; mix well. Sprinkle 1 tablespoon seasoning mixture on chicken pieces; press mixture into chicken pieces with hand. Combine remaining mixture with flour in large plastic bag; set aside.

In large skillet over medium-high heat, heat ½ inch oil to 350°F; adjust heat to maintain temperature. Dredge chicken pieces in seasoned flour; shake off excess. Fry in oil (cook larger pieces first, skin side down) 5 minutes per side or until golden brown. Drain on paper towels.

In large saucepot or Dutch oven, cook bacon 3 to 4 minutes or until it starts to crisp. Stir in onions, celery, bay leaves and 1 teaspoon Tabasco® sauce. Cook 5 minutes; stir frequently. Stir in black-eyed peas, remaining 1 teaspoon onion powder, 3 teaspoons garlic powder, 1½ teaspoons sage and 1 teaspoon thyme.

Cook 2 to 4 minutes or until liquid is absorbed; stir frequently. Add stock, chicken pieces and remaining 1 tablespoon Tabasco® sauce. Simmer, covered, about 1½ to 2 hours or until chicken and black-eyed peas are tender; stir occasionally. Remove and discard bay leaves. Serve with rice.

Makes 8 servings

Cornbread Chicken Pie

1 package (11.5 ounces) refrigerated cornbread twists
2 cups diced cooked chicken
1 cup OCEAN SPRAY® Cran-Fruit™ Crushed Fruit for Chicken
2 cups prepared stuffing
1 package (7 ounces) refrigerated cornbread twists

Preheat oven to 350°F. To make bottom crust, unroll 11.5-ounce package of cornbread twists; flatten with fingers and fit into bottom and side of 9-inch pie plate. Place chicken into crust; top with Cran-Fruit™ Crushed Fruit for Chicken. Spoon in stuffing. To make top crust, unroll 7-ounce package of cornbread twists; flatten with fingers and fit on top of pie. Bake 15 minutes. Cover with aluminum foil; bake 15 minutes. Let stand 5 minutes before serving.   *Makes 4 to 6 servings*

Magically Moist Chicken

Magically Moist Chicken

1 broiler-fryer chicken, cut up
 (2¹/₂ to 3¹/₂ pounds)
¹/₂ cup HELLMANN'S® or
 BEST FOODS® Real, Light or
 Cholesterol Free Reduced
 Calorie Mayonnaise
1¹/₄ cups Italian seasoned dry bread
 crumbs

Brush chicken on all sides with
mayonnaise. Place bread crumbs in
large plastic bag. Add chicken, one
piece at a time; shake to coat well.
Arrange in single layer on rack in
broiler pan. Bake in 425°F oven 40
minutes or until chicken is golden
brown and juices run clear.

Makes 4 servings

Chicken-Broccoli Bake

2 cups chopped cooked broccoli
2 cups cubed cooked chicken
2 cups soft bread cubes
2 cups (8 ounces) shredded process
 sharp American cheese
1 jar (12 ounces) HEINZ® HomeStyle
 Chicken Gravy
¹/₂ cup undiluted evaporated milk
 Dash pepper

In buttered, 9-inch square baking dish,
layer broccoli, chicken, bread cubes and
cheese. In medium bowl, combine
gravy, milk and pepper; pour over
chicken-broccoli mixture. Bake in 375°F
oven 40 minutes. Let stand 5 minutes.

Makes 6 servings

Chicken Picante

3 boneless skinless chicken breasts,
    halved (about 2 pounds)
1/2 cup medium-hot chunky taco
    sauce
1/4 cup Dijon-style mustard
2 tablespoons fresh lime juice
2 tablespoons butter or margarine
    Chopped fresh cilantro (optional)
    Plain yogurt

Combine taco sauce, mustard and lime juice in large bowl. Add chicken, turning to coat. Cover; marinate in refrigerator at least 30 minutes.

Melt butter in large skillet over medium heat until foamy. Remove chicken from marinade; reserve marinade. Add chicken to skillet; cook about 10 minutes or until browned on both sides. Add marinade. Increase heat to medium-high; cook chicken about 5 minutes or until glazed and fork can be inserted into chicken with ease. Remove chicken to serving platter. Pour any remaining sauce over chicken. Garnish with cilantro, if desired. Serve with yogurt. *Makes 6 servings*

Favorite recipe from **National Broiler Council**

Chicken and Sausage Sauté

1 pound sweet Italian sausage
1 pound chicken tenders
1 small onion, thinly sliced
1 red bell pepper, thinly sliced
1 teaspoon dried cilantro leaves
1 tub (12 ounces) OCEAN SPRAY®
    Cran-Fruit™ Crushed Fruit for
    Chicken

Remove sausage from casing. Crumble meat. Cook sausage in large skillet until it is no longer pink. Remove sausage from pan; set aside. In same skillet, cook chicken, onion, red pepper and cilantro until chicken is no longer pink in center and onion and pepper have softened. Add sausage; cook until heated through. Serve with Cran-Fruit™ Crushed Fruit for Chicken.

Makes 4 to 6 servings

Chicken in a Skillet

2 tablespoons vegetable oil
1 broiler-fryer chicken, cut up
    (2 1/2 to 3 pounds)
1 can (14 1/2 ounces) whole peeled
    tomatoes, drained and chopped
    (reserve juice)
1 envelope LIPTON® Onion Recipe
    Soup Mix
1/3 cup water

In large skillet, heat oil over medium-high heat. Brown chicken; drain. Add tomatoes, onion recipe soup mix blended with water and reserved juice. Simmer, covered, stirring occasionally, 45 minutes or until chicken is tender and juices run clear. *Makes 4 servings*

Microwave Directions: Omit oil. In 3-quart casserole, microwave chicken, uncovered, at HIGH 12 minutes, rearranging once; drain. Add tomatoes, onion recipe soup mix blended with water and reserved juice. Microwave, covered, at HIGH 14 minutes or until chicken is tender and juices run clear, rearranging chicken once. Let stand, covered, 5 minutes before serving.

Chicken Picante

Chicken and Zucchini Lasagne

8 lasagne noodles
3 cups (¼-inch-thick) zucchini slices
    (about 2 medium zucchini)
1 tablespoon butter or margarine
1 jar (12 ounces) HEINZ® HomeStyle
    Chicken Gravy
⅔ cup half-and-half or milk
⅓ cup grated Romano or Parmesan
    cheese
½ teaspoon dried basil leaves,
    crushed
¼ teaspoon dried thyme leaves,
    crushed
1½ cups ricotta cheese
1 egg, slightly beaten
3 green onions, sliced
2 tablespoons chopped fresh parsley
2 cups cubed cooked chicken
1 cup (4 ounces) shredded
    mozzarella cheese
¼ cup grated Romano or Parmesan
    cheese
¼ cup plain dry bread crumbs
1 tablespoon butter or margarine,
    melted
    Paprika

Cook lasagne noodles following package directions; set aside.

In large skillet, lightly sauté zucchini in 1 tablespoon butter. In medium bowl, combine gravy, half-and-half, ⅓ cup Romano cheese, basil and thyme. In separate medium bowl, combine ricotta cheese, egg, green onions and parsley.

Pour one third of gravy mixture into 3-quart oblong baking dish. Arrange 4 cooked lasagne noodles over gravy mixture. Cover noodles with half of *each*: ricotta mixture, zucchini, chicken, mozzarella cheese. Spoon one third of gravy mixture over cheese; repeat layers, ending with remaining gravy mixture. In small bowl, combine ¼ cup Romano cheese, bread crumbs and melted butter; sprinkle over top of baking dish and dust with paprika.

Bake in 350°F oven 45 minutes; let stand 10 minutes before serving.

Makes 6 to 8 servings

Chicken-Macaroni Casserole

1 package (7 ounces) CREAMETTES®
    Elbow Macaroni (2 cups
    uncooked)
2 slices bacon, cut up
2 cans (10¾ ounces each) condensed
    cream of mushroom soup
¾ cup milk
2 teaspoons sugar
1 clove garlic, minced
2 tablespoons vinegar
2 cans (5 ounces each) chunk
    chicken
1 cup sliced carrots, cooked crisp-
    tender
1 cup (4 ounces) shredded sharp
    Cheddar cheese
1 cup frozen peas, thawed, drained

Prepare macaroni according to package directions; drain. Cook and stir bacon in medium skillet over medium-high heat until bacon is browned. Remove from skillet with slotted spoon; drain on paper towels. Stir soup, milk, sugar and garlic into drippings. Blend in vinegar.

Combine bacon, soup mixture and remaining ingredients in large bowl. Pour into 2-quart casserole. Cover and bake at 350°F, 30 minutes or until heated through. *Makes 6 to 8 servings*

Double-Coated Chicken

Double-Coated Chicken

7 cups KELLOGG'S®
    CORN FLAKES® Cereal,
    crushed to 1³⁄₄ cups
1 egg
1 cup skim milk
¹⁄₂ cup all-purpose flour
¹⁄₂ teaspoon salt
¹⁄₄ teaspoon pepper
3 pounds broiler-fryer chicken
    pieces, washed and patted dry
3 tablespoons margarine, melted

1. Measure crushed Kellogg's® Corn Flakes® cereal into shallow dish or pan. Set aside.

2. In small mixing bowl, beat egg and milk slightly. Add flour, salt and pepper. Mix until smooth. Dip chicken in batter. Coat in crumbs. Place in single layer, skin side up, in foil-lined, shallow baking pan. Drizzle with margarine.

3. Bake in preheated 350°F oven about 1 hour or until chicken is tender and juices run clear. Do not cover pan or turn chicken while baking.

Makes 6 servings

Dairyland Confetti Chicken

Casserole
- 1 cup diced carrots
- ¾ cup chopped onion
- ½ cup diced celery
- ¼ cup chicken broth
- 1 can (10½ ounces) cream of chicken soup
- 1 cup dairy sour cream
- 3 cups cubed cooked chicken
- ½ cup sliced mushrooms
- 1 teaspoon Worcestershire sauce
- 1 teaspoon salt
- ⅛ teaspoon black pepper

Confetti Topping
- 1 cup sifted all-purpose flour
- 2 teaspoons baking powder
- ½ teaspoon salt
- 2 eggs, slightly beaten
- ½ cup milk
- 1 tablespoon chopped green bell pepper
- 1 tablespoon chopped pimiento
- 1¼ cups (5 ounces) shredded Wisconsin Cheddar cheese, divided

For Casserole, in medium saucepan, combine carrots, onion, celery and chicken broth. Simmer over medium heat 20 minutes. In 3-quart casserole, mix soup, sour cream, chicken, mushrooms, Worcestershire sauce, 1 teaspoon salt and black pepper. Add simmered vegetables and broth; mix well.

For Confetti Topping, in mixing bowl, combine flour, baking powder and ½ teaspoon salt. Add eggs, milk, bell pepper, pimiento and 1 cup cheese. Mix just until blended. Drop tablespoons of topping onto casserole; bake in 350°F oven 40 to 45 minutes or until golden brown. Sprinkle with remaining ¼ cup cheese; return to oven to melt cheese. Garnish as desired.

Makes 6 to 8 servings

Favorite recipe from **Wisconsin Milk Marketing Board** © *1992*

Spicy Baked Chicken

- 2 broiler-fryer chickens, cut up (2½ to 3 pounds each)
- 2 chicken bouillon cubes
- 1 cup boiling water
- 4 teaspoons Worcestershire sauce
- 2 cloves garlic, minced
- 2 teaspoons curry powder
- 2 teaspoons dried oregano leaves
- 1 teaspoon salt
- 1 teaspoon dry mustard
- 1 teaspoon paprika
- ½ teaspoon TABASCO® Pepper Sauce

Preheat oven to 375°F. In large, shallow baking pan, place chicken pieces, skin side down. In measuring cup, dissolve bouillon cubes in boiling water. Add Worcestershire sauce, garlic, curry powder, oregano, salt, mustard, paprika and Tabasco® sauce; mix well. Spoon mixture over chicken; bake 30 minutes. Turn chicken over; baste with pan juices. Bake 20 to 30 minutes or until chicken is tender and juices run clear.

Makes 8 servings

Dairyland Confetti Chicken

Balsamic Chicken and Peppers

Balsamic Chicken and Peppers

2 small boneless skinless chicken breasts, halved (about 1 pound)
1 tablespoon all-purpose flour
1 teaspoon ground coriander
½ teaspoon salt (optional)
1 tablespoon olive oil
1 small onion, cut into thin wedges
2 cloves garlic, minced
1 small red bell pepper, cut into short, thin strips
½ cup reduced-sodium chicken broth
½ cup no-salt-added tomato sauce
2 tablespoons balsamic vinegar, divided*
1½ teaspoons dried basil leaves, crushed
1½ cups UNCLE BEN'S® Rice In An Instant
¼ cup thinly sliced green onions with tops
Freshly ground black pepper

Pound chicken to ½-inch thickness. Rub with combined flour, coriander and salt. Brown chicken in oil in 10-inch skillet over medium-high heat 2 minutes on each side. Remove and reserve. Add onion, garlic and red pepper to skillet; cook and stir 2 minutes. Add broth, tomato sauce, 1 tablespoon vinegar and basil. Return chicken to skillet; spoon sauce over chicken. Cover; cook over low heat 8 minutes or until chicken is tender and juices run clear.

Meanwhile, cook rice according to package directions, adding green onions with rice. When chicken is cooked through, stir in remaining 1 tablespoon vinegar; cook, uncovered, over high heat until sauce has thickened. Serve chicken over rice; top with sauce. Sprinkle with black pepper to taste.

Makes 4 servings

*Substitute red wine vinegar for the balsamic vinegar. Decrease amount to 1 tablespoon; add to skillet with tomato sauce.

Herbed Baked Chicken

¾ cup QUAKER® Oat Bran hot
   cereal, uncooked
¼ teaspoon garlic powder
¼ teaspoon pepper
¼ teaspoon salt (optional)
1 egg white, slightly beaten
1 tablespoon water
3 small boneless skinless chicken
   breasts, halved (about 1 pound)
2 tablespoons liquid vegetable oil
   margarine
¼ cup snipped fresh parsley *or* 1½
   teaspoons parsley flakes

Heat oven to 350°F. In shallow dish, combine oat bran, garlic powder, pepper and salt; mix well. In another shallow dish, lightly beat egg white and water. Dip chicken into egg mixture, then coat with oat bran mixture. Place on wire rack in 15 × 10-inch, foil-lined baking pan. Drizzle with margarine.

Bake 45 to 50 minutes or until chicken is tender and coating is lightly browned. Remove chicken to serving platter. Top with parsley. Squeeze lemon wedge over chicken before serving, if desired.   *Makes 6 servings*

Tip: To snip fresh parsley, rinse with cool water; dry thoroughly. Remove stems; place parsley tops in short plastic cup. Using kitchen shears, snip parsley until well chopped.

Herbed Baked Chicken

Baked Chicken Reuben

**4 boneless skinless chicken breasts,
    halved (about 2½ pounds)**
¼ teaspoon salt
⅛ teaspoon pepper
**1 can (16 ounces) sauerkraut, well
    drained**
**4 slices Swiss cheese (6 × 4 inches
    each)**
**1¼ cups prepared Thousand Island
    salad dressing**

Preheat oven to 325°F. Place chicken in
single layer in greased baking pan.
Sprinkle with salt and pepper. Spoon
sauerkraut over chicken. Arrange cheese
slices over sauerkraut. Pour dressing
evenly over top. Cover pan with
aluminum foil. Bake about 1½ hours or
until fork can be inserted into chicken
with ease.   *Makes 6 to 8 servings*

Favorite recipe from **National Broiler Council**

Ortega® Salsa Chicken

**2 boneless chicken breasts, halved
    (about 1¼ pounds)**
1 tablespoon vegetable oil
**1 jar (12 ounces) ORTEGA® Thick 'n
    Chunky Salsa**

In large skillet over medium-high heat,
brown chicken in hot oil; drain fat. Add
salsa; bring to a boil. Reduce heat to
low. Cover; simmer 15 minutes or until
chicken is tender and juices run clear,
turning once.   *Makes 4 servings*

Perfect Chicken and Pork Pie

**2 PET-RITZ® Deep-Dish Pie Crust
    Shells**
½ pound pork sausage
¼ cup butter or margarine
⅓ cup all-purpose flour
1 teaspoon celery seed
½ teaspoon paprika
½ teaspoon poultry seasoning
¼ teaspoon curry powder
¼ teaspoon salt
⅛ teaspoon pepper
**1 can (14½ ounces) ready-to-serve
    chicken broth**
⅔ cup milk
2 cups cubed cooked chicken
**1 package (10 ounces) frozen peas,
    thawed**

Invert one pie crust onto waxed paper.
Let thaw until flat. Preheat oven and
baking sheet to 375°F. Brown sausage in
large skillet over medium-high heat;
drain sausage on paper towels. Melt
butter in same skillet over medium
heat. Blend in flour, celery seed,
paprika, poultry seasoning, curry
powder, salt and pepper. Gradually stir
in broth and milk. Cook until
thickened, stirring constantly; cook 1
minute more. Add chicken, sausage and
peas. Pour into pie crust shell. Cover
with flattened crust. Seal edge. Cut slits
for steam to escape. Bake on preheated
baking sheet 45 to 50 minutes or until
golden brown.   *Makes 6 servings*

Baked Chicken Reuben

Creamy Chicken Hash

1 small bell pepper, chopped
¼ cup chopped onion
2 tablespoons butter, melted
3 cups IDAHO® frozen Southern
    Style Hash Brown Potatoes
2 cups cubed cooked chicken
¾ cup chicken gravy
¼ cup milk
2 to 3 teaspoons prepared
    horseradish
½ teaspoon salt
¼ teaspoon TABASCO® Pepper Sauce

Cook pepper and onion in melted butter in large skillet over medium heat 3 minutes or until tender, stirring frequently. Remove from heat. Add remaining ingredients; toss to mix well. Spoon into 2-quart casserole. Bake in preheated 350°F oven 45 minutes or until heated through.

Makes 4 servings

Camp Fried Chicken and Rice

1½ pounds boneless skinless chicken
    thighs, cut into chunks
2¼ cups water
3 chicken-flavored bouillon cubes
1 cup long-grain rice
1 can (4 ounces) mushroom stems
    and pieces, drained
½ cup all-purpose flour
¾ teaspoon salt (optional)
½ teaspoon pepper
⅔ cup vegetable oil

In medium saucepan, bring water and bouillon to boil over high heat; stir to dissolve bouillon. Add rice; reduce heat. Cover; cook until rice is done and liquid is absorbed, 20 minutes. Stir in mushrooms; cover.

While rice cooks, combine flour, salt and pepper. Add chicken; turn to coat evenly. In skillet, cook chicken in hot oil over medium-high heat, turning occasionally, 10 minutes or until fork can be inserted into chicken with ease. Remove from heat; drain oil. Stir in rice-mushroom mixture.

Makes 4 servings

*Favorite recipe from **National Broiler Council***

Chicken Santa Fe

¼ cup all-purpose flour
2½ pounds boneless skinless chicken
    breasts, halved
3 tablespoons olive oil
3½ cups (two 14½-ounce cans)
    CONTADINA® Stewed Tomatoes
1½ cups coarsely chopped onion
2 cloves garlic, crushed
½ cup mild green chili salsa
¼ teaspoon salt
2 cups hot cooked rice (optional)
    Sour cream
1 small avocado, halved, peeled,
    pitted and cut into 16 slices
    Fresh cilantro leaves

Place flour in shallow dish; dredge chicken in flour to coat evenly. In 12-inch skillet over medium-high heat, sauté chicken in hot oil 5 minutes on each side or until golden brown. Keep warm; set aside.

In medium bowl, combine stewed tomatoes, onion, garlic, salsa and salt. Pour over chicken in skillet. Cover; simmer 20 minutes, stirring occasionally. Remove cover; simmer 15 minutes or until chicken is tender and juices run clear. Serve chicken over rice on individual plates; top with sauce. Top each serving with dollop of sour cream and 2 avocado slices; garnish with cilantro.

Makes 8 servings

Chicken with Potatoes & Peppers

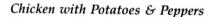

¼ cup WISH-BONE® Italian
    Dressing
1 broiler-fryer chicken, cut up
    (2½ to 3 pounds)
1 can (28 ounces) whole peeled
    tomatoes, undrained, chopped
1 pound all-purpose potatoes, cut
    into chunks
2 medium onions, cut into quarters
2 medium red, green or yellow
    peppers, cut into thin strips
1 tablespoon fresh rosemary leaves
    or 1 teaspoon dried rosemary
    leaves
1 teaspoon dried thyme leaves
1 teaspoon salt
¼ teaspoon black pepper

Preheat oven to 375°F. In large skillet, heat Italian Dressing. Brown chicken over medium-high heat; set aside.

In 13 × 9-inch baking pan, combine remaining ingredients; add chicken and turn to coat. Bake, uncovered, stirring occasionally, 50 minutes or until chicken is done and vegetables are tender. Serve with French or Italian bread, if desired.

Makes 4 servings

•Also terrific with Wish-Bone® Robusto Italian, Blended Italian, Lite Italian or Lite Classic Dijon Vinaigrette Dressing.

Chicken with Potatoes & Peppers

Apple Curry Chicken

2 boneless skinless chicken breasts,
    halved (about 1¼ pounds)
1 cup apple juice, divided
¼ teaspoon salt
    Dash of pepper
1½ cups plain croutons
1 medium apple, chopped
½ cup finely chopped onion
¼ cup raisins
2 teaspoons brown sugar
1 teaspoon curry powder
¾ teaspoon poultry seasoning
⅛ teaspoon garlic powder

Preheat oven to 350°F. Lightly grease shallow baking dish. Arrange chicken in single layer in prepared dish. Combine ¼ cup apple juice, salt and pepper in small bowl; brush entire mixture over chicken. Combine croutons, apple, onion, raisins, brown sugar, curry powder, poultry seasoning and garlic powder in large bowl. Stir in remaining ¾ cup apple juice; spread over chicken. Cover; bake about 45 minutes or until chicken is tender and juices run clear. Garnish as desired.   *Makes 4 servings*

Favorite recipe from **Delmarva Poultry Industry, Inc.**

Chicken Olé

2 tablespoons vegetable oil
1 cup chopped onion
2 cloves garlic, minced
1 can (10½ ounces) tomato purée
1 cup Florida orange juice
3 tablespoons chopped canned green
    chilies
1 teaspoon grated orange peel
1 teaspoon ground cinnamon
½ teaspoon dried thyme leaves,
    crushed
½ teaspoon salt
1 broiler-fryer chicken (2½ to
    3½ pounds)
    Salt and black pepper
8 new potatoes
3 medium red bell peppers, seeded
    and sliced

Preheat oven to 350°F. In large skillet, heat oil over medium heat; cook and stir onion and garlic in oil until tender. Add tomato purée, orange juice, chilies, orange peel, cinnamon, thyme and ½ teaspoon salt. Cook 10 minutes, stirring occasionally.

Meanwhile, sprinkle chicken, inside and out, with salt and black pepper. Place chicken in large baking dish. Peel a narrow strip around each potato. Arrange potatoes around chicken. Pour sauce over all; cover.

Bake 45 minutes. Add red peppers; cover. Bake 45 minutes or until chicken and potatoes are tender.

Makes 4 servings

Favorite recipe from **Florida Department of Citrus**

Apple Curry Chicken

Home-Style Chicken 'n Biscuits

5 slices bacon, fried crisp and
    crumbled
1½ cups (7 ounces) cubed cooked
    chicken
1 package (10 ounces) frozen mixed
    vegetables, thawed and drained
1½ cups (6 ounces) shredded Cheddar
    cheese
2 medium tomatoes, chopped
    (about 1 cup)
1 can (10¾ ounces) condensed cream
    of chicken soup
¾ cup milk
1½ cups biscuit baking mix
⅔ cup milk
1 can (2.8 ounces) DURKEE® French
    Fried Onions

Preheat oven to 400°F. In large bowl,
combine bacon, chicken, mixed
vegetables, *1 cup* cheese, tomatoes, soup
and ¾ cup milk. Pour chicken mixture
into greased 12 × 8-inch baking dish.
Bake, covered, 15 minutes.

Meanwhile, in medium bowl, combine
baking mix, ⅔ cup milk and *½ can*
French Fried Onions to form soft
dough. Spoon biscuit dough in six
mounds around edges of baking dish.
Bake, uncovered, 15 to 20 minutes or
until biscuits are golden brown. Top
biscuits with remaining cheese and
onions; bake 1 to 3 minutes or until
onions are golden brown.

Makes 6 servings

Microwave Directions: Reduce ¾ cup
milk to ½ cup. Combine chicken
mixture as directed; pour into 12 × 8-
inch microwave-safe dish. Microwave,
covered, on HIGH 10 minutes or until
heated through. Stir chicken mixture
halfway through cooking time. Prepare
biscuit dough as directed. Stir casserole;
spoon biscuit dough over hot chicken
mixture as directed. Microwave,
uncovered, on HIGH 7 to 8 minutes or
until biscuits are done. Rotate dish
halfway through cooking time. Top
biscuits with remaining cheese and
onions; microwave, uncovered, on
HIGH 1 minute or until cheese melts.
Let stand 5 minutes before serving.

Peanut Chicken

1 broiler-fryer chicken, cut up
    (about 3 pounds)
2 teaspoons vegetable oil
1 can (14½ ounces) DEL MONTE®
    Original Style Stewed Tomatoes,
    undrained, coarsely chopped
3 tablespoons chunky peanut butter
2 cloves garlic, crushed
1 teaspoon grated gingerroot
1 teaspoon soy sauce
⅛ to ¼ teaspoon crushed red pepper
    flakes

In large skillet over medium-high heat,
brown chicken on all sides in oil about
15 minutes or until chicken is tender
and juices run clear. Drain fat. Set
chicken aside; keep warm.

In same skillet, add tomatoes with juice,
peanut butter, garlic, gingerroot, soy
sauce and red pepper. Simmer
3 minutes. Add chicken; cook 2 minutes
or until heated through, turning once.
Garnish with chopped peanuts and
fresh cilantro, if desired.

Makes 4 to 6 servings

Prep and Cook Time: 28 minutes

Chicken Avocado Melt

Chicken Avocado Melt

2 boneless skinless chicken breasts,
    halved (about 1¼ pounds)
2 tablespoons cornstarch
1 teaspoon ground cumin
1 teaspoon garlic salt
1 egg
1 tablespoon water
⅓ cup yellow cornmeal
3 tablespoons vegetable oil
1 firm ripe avocado, halved, peeled,
    pitted and sliced
1½ cups (6 ounces) shredded
    Monterey Jack cheese
½ cup sour cream
¼ cup sliced green onion tops
¼ cup chopped red bell pepper

Preheat oven to 350°F. Pound chicken between 2 pieces of plastic wrap to ¼-inch thickness. Combine cornstarch, cumin and garlic salt in shallow dish. Add chicken, dredging to coat.

Combine egg and water in small bowl. Place cornmeal in shallow dish. Dip chicken into egg mixture; then roll in cornmeal to coat evenly. Heat oil in large skillet over medium heat. Add chicken; cook 2 minutes on each side or until lightly browned. Remove chicken to shallow baking pan. Arrange avocado slices over chicken; sprinkle with cheese.

Bake about 15 minutes or until fork can be inserted into chicken with ease and cheese melts. Transfer chicken to serving platter. Top with sour cream; sprinkle with onion tops and red pepper.　　　　*Makes 4 servings*

*Favorite recipe from **National Broiler Council***

Hidden Valley Fried Chicken

1 broiler-fryer chicken, cut up
 (2 to 2½ pounds)
1 cup prepared
 HIDDEN VALLEY RANCH®
 Original Ranch® Salad Dressing
¾ cup all-purpose flour
1 teaspoon salt
½ teaspoon freshly ground black
 pepper
 Vegetable oil

Place chicken pieces in shallow baking dish; pour salad dressing over chicken. Cover; refrigerate at least 8 hours. Remove chicken. Shake off excess marinade; discard marinade. Preheat oven to 350°F. On plate, mix flour, salt and pepper; roll chicken in seasoned flour. Heat ½ inch oil in large skillet until small cube of bread dropped into oil browns in 60 seconds or until oil is 375°F. Fry chicken until golden, 5 to 7 minutes on each side; transfer to baking pan. Bake until chicken is tender and juices run clear, about 30 minutes. Serve with corn muffins, if desired.

Serves 4 as a main dish

Skillet Hickory Chicken

1 broiler-fryer chicken, cut up
 (about 3 pounds)
1 tablespoon vegetable oil
1 can (14½ ounces) DEL MONTE®
 Original Style Stewed Tomatoes,
 chopped
½ cup chopped onion
2 cloves garlic, crushed
¼ cup apricot jam
1½ teaspoons chili powder
⅛ to ¼ teaspoon liquid hickory
 smoke seasoning

In large skillet, cook chicken on all sides in oil over medium-high heat until chicken is browned and juices run clear, about 20 minutes; drain fat. In saucepan, combine tomatoes, onion, garlic, jam, chili powder and hickory seasoning. Bring to a boil. Reduce heat; simmer 10 minutes. Pour over cooked chicken; simmer 3 to 5 minutes, turning occasionally. *Makes 4 to 6 servings*

Prep and Cook Time: 30 minutes

Healthful Chicken Casserole

1 broiler-fryer chicken, cooked,
 skinned, boned and chopped
 (about 3 pounds)
1 package (10 ounces) frozen
 spinach
¼ cup finely chopped onion
½ teaspoon garlic powder, divided
8 ounces mushrooms, sliced
2 tablespoons diet margarine,
 melted
1 cup (4 ounces) shredded skim
 mozzarella cheese

Cook spinach according to package directions, eliminating salt; drain. Stir onion into spinach. Arrange spinach mixture in bottom of 1½-quart baking dish; sprinkle with ¼ teaspoon garlic powder. Arrange mushrooms on spinach; drizzle with margarine. Place chicken on mushrooms; sprinkle with remaining ¼ teaspoon garlic powder. Top with mozzarella cheese. Bake in 350°F oven 30 minutes or until fork can be inserted into chicken with ease.

Makes 6 servings

*Favorite recipe from **National Broiler Council***

Hidden Valley Fried Chicken

Teen's Pizza Chicken

Teen's Pizza Chicken

5 broiler-fryer chicken quarters
1 teaspoon garlic salt
½ teaspoon pepper
1 jar (15½ ounces) pizza sauce
¼ cup sour cream
1 can (4 ounces) mushroom stems
  and pieces, drained
½ teaspoon dried oregano leaves
1½ cups (6 ounces) shredded
  mozzarella cheese

Line shallow baking pan with foil; spray foil with vegetable cooking spray. (Pan should be large enough so that all chicken pieces fit in one layer.) Arrange chicken on foil; sprinkle with garlic salt and pepper. Set oven temperature control to *broil* (450°F); arrange oven rack so chicken is about 6 inches from heat. Broil chicken 15 minutes or until skin is browned. (Do not turn chicken over.)

Meanwhile, in medium bowl, combine pizza sauce, sour cream, mushrooms and oregano. Remove chicken from oven; change oven temperature control to *bake* (350°F). Pour sauce over chicken; bake 30 minutes or until fork can be inserted into chicken with ease. Remove chicken from oven; sprinkle cheese over each piece. Return to oven for 5 minutes to melt cheese.   *Makes 5 servings*

*Favorite recipe from **National Broiler Council***

Chicken and Vegetable Pie

3¹/₃ cups water, divided
1¹/₂ cups cubed potatoes (¹/₂-inch
    cubes)
  ³/₄ teaspoon salt
  3 tablespoons CRISCO® Oil
  1 small onion, thinly sliced
  2 tablespoons plus 1 teaspoon all-
    purpose flour
  1 tablespoon instant chicken
    bouillon granules
  1 teaspoon parsley flakes
  ¹/₄ to ¹/₂ teaspoon dried thyme leaves
  ¹/₄ teaspoon pepper
  1 cup milk
1¹/₂ cups chopped cooked chicken
  ¹/₂ cup frozen corn
  ¹/₂ cup frozen green peas
  1 can (4 ounces) mushroom stems
    and pieces, drained
    Classic Crisco® Double Crust
    (recipe follows)

1. Combine 3 cups water, potatoes and salt in 2-quart saucepan. Heat to boiling over medium high heat; reduce heat. Cover; simmer about 10 minutes or until potatoes are tender. Drain. Set aside.

2. Heat Crisco® Oil in medium saucepan over medium heat. Add onion; sauté until tender. Stir in flour, bouillon granules, parsley flakes, thyme and pepper. Blend in milk and remaining ¹/₃ cup water. Cook over medium heat, stirring constantly, until thickened and bubbly. Remove from heat. Add potatoes, chicken, corn, peas and mushrooms. Stir to break apart corn and peas. Set aside.

3. Preheat oven to 425°F. Prepare Classic Crisco® Double Crust. Roll and fit crust into 9-inch pie plate as directed. Fill with chicken mixture. Top with remaining crust as directed; flute edges. Cut slits in top. Place in oven. *Immediately reduce temperature to 325°F.* Bake at 325°F, 45 to 60 minutes or until filling is hot and crust is flaky.

Makes 4 to 6 servings

Classic Crisco® Double Crust

  2 cups all-purpose flour
  1 teaspoon salt
  ³/₄ cup CRISCO® Shortening
  5 to 8 tablespoons cold water

1. Spoon flour into measuring cup and level. Combine flour and salt in medium bowl.

2. Cut in Crisco® using pastry blender (or 2 knives) until all flour is blended to form pea-sized chunks.

3. Sprinkle with water, 1 tablespoon at a time. Toss lightly with fork until dough forms ball.

4. Divide dough in half. Roll each half separately. Transfer bottom crust to pie plate. Trim edge even with pie plate.

5. Add filling to unbaked pie crust. Moisten pastry edge with water. Lift top crust onto filled pie. Trim ¹/₂ inch beyond edge of pie plate. Fold top edge under bottom crust. Flute. Cut slits in top crust to allow steam to escape. Bake according to recipe directions.

Makes one 9-inch double crust

Gingered Chicken Thighs

  1 tablespoon peanut or vegetable oil
  ½ teaspoon hot chili oil
  8 chicken thighs (1½ to 2 pounds)
  2 cloves garlic, minced
  ¼ cup sweet and sour sauce
  1 tablespoon soy sauce
  2 teaspoons minced fresh ginger
    Cilantro and orange peel for
    garnish

Heat large, nonstick skillet over medium-high heat until hot. Add peanut oil and chili oil; heat until hot. Cook chicken thighs, skin side down, in hot oil 4 minutes or until golden brown. Reduce heat to low; turn chicken over. Cover; cook 15 to 18 minutes or until juices run clear. Spoon off fat.

Increase heat to medium. Stir in garlic; cook 2 minutes. Combine sweet and sour sauce, soy sauce and ginger in small bowl. Brush half of mixture over chicken; turn chicken over and brush with remaining mixture. Cook 5 minutes, turning once more, until sauce has thickened, chicken is tender and juices run clear. Transfer chicken to serving platter; pour sauce evenly over chicken. Garnish with cilantro and orange peel.   *Makes 4 servings*

Versatile Chicken

  ¾ cup BORDEN® or
    MEADOW GOLD® Buttermilk
  1 tablespoon WYLER'S® or
    STEERO® Chicken-Flavor Instant
    Bouillon
  ½ teaspoon oregano leaves, optional
  3 pounds chicken pieces
  1 cup unsifted flour
  1 teaspoon paprika
  ¼ cup margarine or butter, melted

In large bowl, combine buttermilk, bouillon and oregano; let stand 10 minutes. Stir. Add chicken; stir to coat. Let stand 30 minutes to blend flavors. In plastic bag, combine flour and paprika. Add chicken, a few pieces at a time; shake to coat.

Place in 13×9-inch baking dish. Drizzle with margarine. Bake at 350°F for 1 hour or until golden. Refrigerate leftovers.   *Makes 4 to 6 servings*

Tip: To fry chicken, omit margarine; fry in vegetable oil.

Brown Rice Chicken Bake

  3 cups cooked brown rice
  1 package (10 ounces) frozen green
    peas
  2 cups cubed cooked chicken breast
  ½ cup cholesterol-free, reduced-
    calorie mayonnaise
  ⅓ cup toasted slivered almonds
    (optional)*
  2 teaspoons soy sauce
  ¼ teaspoon ground black pepper
  ¼ teaspoon garlic powder
  ¼ teaspoon dried tarragon leaves
    Vegetable cooking spray

Combine rice, peas, chicken, mayonnaise, almonds, soy sauce and seasonings in bowl. Transfer to 3-quart baking dish coated with cooking spray. Cover and bake at 350°F for 15 to 20 minutes.   *Makes 6 servings*

*See page 42 for directions for toasting almonds.

Favorite recipe from **USA Rice Council**

Gingered Chicken Thighs

Chicken Fiesta

2½ to 3 pounds chicken pieces
Salt
Pepper
Paprika
2 tablespoons butter or margarine, melted
¼ pound pork sausage
¾ cup sliced celery
¾ cup sliced green onions, including tops
3 cups cooked rice
1 can (12 ounces) whole kernel corn with peppers
2 teaspoons lemon juice

Season chicken with salt, pepper and paprika. Brown in melted butter in large skillet over medium heat. Drain chicken on paper towels; set aside. Cook sausage, celery and onions in same skillet over medium-high heat until vegetables are tender, stirring frequently. Add rice, corn and lemon juice; mix well. Pour into buttered, shallow baking dish. Arrange chicken on top of rice mixture, pushing slightly into rice mixture. Cover with foil. Bake at 350°F for 30 to 40 minutes or until chicken is tender. *Makes 6 servings*

Favorite recipe from **USA Rice Council**

Chicken Fiesta

Sweet and Sour Chicken Balls

1 pound ground chicken
1 egg, slightly beaten
1 clove garlic, minced
$\frac{1}{2}$ teaspoon salt
$\frac{1}{4}$ teaspoon black pepper
5 tablespoons all-purpose flour, divided
3 tablespoons canola or vegetable oil
1 can (14 ounces) pineapple chunks in juice, undrained
1 chicken bouillon cube
1 green bell pepper, sliced into 1$\frac{1}{2}$-inch pieces
2 tablespoons cornstarch
2 tablespoons sugar
1 teaspoon ground ginger
$\frac{1}{4}$ cup vinegar
2 tablespoons soy sauce

In medium bowl, mix together egg, garlic, salt and black pepper. Add ground chicken and 2 tablespoons flour. On waxed paper, sprinkle remaining 3 tablespoons flour. Drop chicken mixture by heaping teaspoons onto floured waxed paper; roll in flour to form balls.

In nonstick skillet, heat canola oil over high heat; add chicken balls and cook, turning, until browned and no longer pink in centers, about 6 minutes. Remove chicken balls; drain on paper towels. Drain oil from skillet, reserving 1 tablespoon drippings.

Drain juice from pineapple chunks into measuring cup; add water to make 1 cup liquid. Add bouillon to pineapple juice; stir to dissolve.

In skillet over low heat, cook pineapple chunks and green pepper about 2 minutes, stirring constantly. In small bowl, combine cornstarch, sugar and ginger; stir in vinegar and soy sauce

until smooth. To skillet, add pineapple juice mixture and cornstarch mixture, stirring and cooking until clear and thickened, about 5 minutes.

Arrange chicken balls over sauce; serve with rice and crisp Chinese noodles, if desired. *Makes 6 servings*

*Favorite recipe from **National Broiler Council***

Creole Chicken Thighs

8 skinless broiler-fryer chicken thighs
2 tablespoons butter or margarine
$\frac{1}{2}$ pound mushrooms, sliced
1 medium onion, chopped
$\frac{1}{2}$ cup chopped green bell pepper
$\frac{1}{2}$ cup thinly sliced celery
2 cloves garlic, minced
1 can (16 ounces) tomatoes, cut up
$\frac{1}{2}$ teaspoon salt
$\frac{1}{2}$ teaspoon sugar
$\frac{1}{2}$ teaspoon dried thyme leaves, crumbled
$\frac{1}{2}$ teaspoon hot pepper sauce
2 bay leaves
2 cups hot cooked rice

In skillet, melt butter over medium-high heat. Add mushrooms, onion, pepper, celery and garlic. Cook, stirring constantly, about 3 minutes or until onion is translucent, but not brown. Stir in tomatoes, salt, sugar, thyme, pepper sauce and bay leaves. Add chicken, spooning sauce over chicken. Cook, covered, over medium heat about 35 minutes or until chicken is tender and juices run clear. Remove and discard bay leaves. Serve chicken and sauce over rice. *Makes 4 servings*

*Favorite recipe from **Delmarva Poultry Industry, Inc.***

Chicken with Lime Butter

3 boneless skinless chicken breasts, halved (about 2 pounds)
$1/2$ teaspoon salt
$1/2$ teaspoon pepper
$1/3$ cup vegetable oil
   Juice of 1 lime
$1/2$ cup butter
 1 teaspoon minced fresh chives
$1/2$ teaspoon dried dill weed

Sprinkle chicken with salt and pepper. Heat oil in large skillet over medium heat. Add chicken; cook until lightly browned, about 3 minutes on each side. Reduce heat to low. Cover; cook 10 minutes or until fork can be inserted into chicken with ease. Remove chicken to serving platter; keep warm.

Drain oil from skillet. Add lime juice; cook over low heat until juice begins to bubble, about 1 minute. Add butter, 1 tablespoon at a time, stirring until butter becomes opaque and forms a thickened sauce. Remove from heat; stir in chives and dill. Spoon sauce over chicken; serve immediately. Garnish as desired. *Makes 6 servings*

Favorite recipe from **National Broiler Council**

Chicken and Red Rice

$2/3$ cup uncooked rice
 1 cup chopped green bell pepper
 1 can (2.8 ounces) DURKEE® French Fried Onions
 2 boneless skinless chicken breasts, halved (about $1^1/4$ pounds)
 1 jar ($15^1/2$ ounces) spaghetti sauce with mushrooms
$1^1/4$ cups water

Preheat oven to 375°F. In 12 × 8-inch baking dish, combine uncooked rice, green pepper and $1/2$ *can* French Fried Onions. Arrange chicken breasts over rice mixture. In medium bowl, combine spaghetti sauce and water; pour over chicken and rice. Bake, covered, 50 minutes or until chicken is tender and rice is done. Top chicken with remaining onions; bake, uncovered, 3 minutes or until onions are golden brown. *Makes 4 servings*

Microwave Directions: Reduce water to 1 cup. In 12 × 8-inch microwave-safe dish, combine uncooked rice and water. Microwave, covered, on HIGH 10 minutes, stirring rice halfway through cooking time. Stir green pepper and $1/2$ *can* onions into rice. Arrange chicken over rice with meatiest parts toward edges of dish. Pour spaghetti sauce over chicken and rice. Microwave, covered, on HIGH 10 minutes, stirring rice halfway through cooking time. Rearrange chicken; rotate dish. Microwave, covered, on HIGH 9 to 10 minutes or until chicken is tender and rice is done. Stir rice halfway through cooking time. Top chicken with remaining onions; microwave, uncovered, on HIGH 1 minute. Let stand 5 minutes before serving.

Chicken with Lime Butter

Chicken Milano

Chicken Milano

2 cloves garlic, minced
2 boneless skinless chicken breasts,
    halved (about 1¼ pounds)
½ teaspoon dried basil leaves,
    crushed
⅛ teaspoon crushed red pepper
    flakes (optional)
  Salt and black pepper
1 tablespoon olive oil
1 can (14½ ounces) DEL MONTE®
    Italian Style Stewed Tomatoes*
1 can (16 ounces) DEL MONTE® Cut
    Green Italian Beans or Blue
    Lake Cut Green Beans, drained
¼ cup whipping cream

Rub garlic over chicken. Sprinkle with basil and red pepper. Season with salt and black pepper. In skillet, brown chicken in oil over medium-high heat. Stir in tomatoes. Cover; simmer 5 minutes. Uncover; reduce heat to medium and cook 8 to 10 minutes or until liquid is slightly thickened and chicken is tender. Stir in green beans and cream; heat through. *Do not boil.*
Makes 4 servings

Prep and Cook Time: 25 minutes

*Substitute Del Monte® Original Style Stewed Tomatoes for the Italian Style Stewed Tomatoes.

Farmer's Chicken Stew

1 stewing chicken, cut into pieces
    (about 5 pounds)
2 cups water
3 small onions, cut into halves
5 whole cloves
1 bay leaf
2 teaspoons salt
1½ teaspoons paprika
¼ teaspoon pepper
2 cups carrots cut diagonally into
    ½-inch slices
2 cups celery cut diagonally into
    ½-inch slices
1 package (10 ounces) frozen peas
    Pimiento Cheese Biscuits (recipe
    follows)
½ cup all-purpose flour
2 cups milk

Place chicken, water, onions, cloves, bay leaf, salt, paprika and pepper in 4-quart Dutch oven. Bring to a boil over high heat. Reduce heat to low. Cover; simmer 2½ to 3 hours or until chicken is tender. Remove and discard cloves and bay leaf. Add vegetables; bring to a boil over high heat. Reduce heat to low. Cover; simmer 15 to 20 minutes or until vegetables are tender. Meanwhile, prepare Pimiento Cheese Biscuits.

Drain broth from Dutch oven; reserve. Skim off excess fat. Pour 3 cups broth into saucepan. (If necessary, add water to measure 3 cups.) Blend flour and milk in small bowl until smooth. Gradually stir into hot broth. Bring to a boil over medium heat, stirring constantly until gravy is thickened. Pour gravy over chicken and vegetables in Dutch oven; heat through. Garnish with additional paprika, if desired. Serve with Pimiento Cheese Biscuits.

Makes 6 servings

Pimiento Cheese Biscuits: Combine 2 cups buttermilk biscuit mix, 1 cup (4 ounces) shredded sharp Cheddar cheese, 2 tablespoons drained chopped pimiento and ¼ teaspoon crushed dried oregano leaves in medium bowl. Add ⅔ cup milk; mix until soft dough is formed. Drop by tablespoonfuls onto lightly buttered baking sheet. Bake in preheated 425°F oven 10 to 12 minutes or until lightly browned. Serve warm with butter. Makes 12 biscuits.

*Favorite recipe from **American Dairy Association***

Crunchy Almond Chicken Cutlets

1 cup plain fresh bread crumbs
1 cup blanched slivered almonds,*
    toasted and finely chopped
2 tablespoons chopped fresh parsley
½ teaspoon ground ginger
¼ teaspoon salt
⅛ teaspoon pepper
3 boneless chicken breasts, halved
    (about 2 pounds)
1 cup (8 ounces) WISH-BONE®
    Creamy Italian or Lite Creamy
    Italian Dressing

Preheat oven to 350°F. In medium bowl, combine bread crumbs, almonds, parsley, ginger, salt and pepper. Dip chicken into Creamy Italian Dressing; roll in bread crumb mixture to coat evenly. In large, shallow baking pan, arrange chicken. Bake, uncovered, 20 minutes or until chicken is tender and juices run clear. *Makes 6 servings*

*See page 42 for directions for toasting almonds.

Chicken in French Onion Sauce

1 package (10 ounces) frozen baby
  carrots, thawed and drained *or*
  4 medium carrots, cut into strips
  (about 2 cups)
2 cups sliced mushrooms
½ cup thinly sliced celery
1 can (2.8 ounces) DURKEE® French
  Fried Onions
2 boneless skinless chicken breasts,
  halved (about 1¼ pounds)
¾ cup prepared chicken bouillon
½ cup white wine
½ teaspoon DURKEE® Garlic Salt
¼ teaspoon DURKEE® Ground Black
  Pepper
  DURKEE® Paprika

Preheat oven to 375°F. In 12 × 8-inch
baking dish, combine vegetables and
½ *can* French Fried Onions. Arrange
chicken breasts on vegetables. In small
bowl, combine bouillon, wine, garlic
salt and pepper; pour over chicken and
vegetables. Sprinkle chicken with
paprika. Bake, covered, 35 minutes or
until chicken is tender and juices run
clear. Baste chicken with wine sauce;
top with remaining onions. Bake,
uncovered, 3 minutes or until onions
are golden brown.   *Makes 4 servings*

Microwave Directions: In 12 × 8-inch
microwave-safe dish, combine
vegetables and ½ *can* onions. Arrange
chicken breasts, skinned side down,
along sides of dish. Prepare wine
mixture as directed, *except* reduce
bouillon to ⅓ cup; pour over chicken
and vegetables. Microwave, covered, on
HIGH 6 minutes. Turn chicken breasts
over; sprinkle with paprika. Stir
vegetables and rotate dish. Microwave,
covered, on HIGH 7 to 9 minutes or

until chicken is tender and juices run
clear. Baste chicken with wine sauce;
top with remaining onions. Microwave,
uncovered, on HIGH 1 minute. Let
stand 5 minutes before serving.

Keam's Canyon Chicken

4 cups tortilla chips
1 broiler-fryer chicken, cut up (3 to
  3½ pounds)
¼ cup butter or margarine, melted
1 package (1¼ ounces) taco
  seasoning mix
2 to 3 cups shredded iceberg lettuce
½ cup sour cream
1 medium avocado
1 lemon, cut into wedges
  Prepared green chili salsa

Preheat oven to 350°F. Place tortilla
chips in blender or food processor
container; process to make coarse
crumbs. (Or place chips in heavy plastic
bag; crush with rolling pin.) Place
crumbs on large plate. Rinse chicken;
pat dry. Combine butter and seasoning
mix in pie plate. Roll each piece of
chicken in butter mixture, then coat
with crumbs. Arrange chicken pieces,
skin side up, slightly apart in 13 × 9-inch
baking pan.

Bake, uncovered, 1 hour or until
chicken is tender and juices run clear.
Arrange chicken on bed of shredded
lettuce; top with sour cream. Peel, pit
and slice avocado. Garnish chicken with
avocado and lemon wedges. Serve with
salsa.   *Makes 4 servings*

Chicken in French Onion Sauce

Chicken Timatar

6 skinless chicken leg quarters
¼ cup vegetable oil
2 medium onions, chopped
6 cloves garlic, very finely chopped
4 whole cardamom pods *or* ¼
　　teaspoon ground cardamom
1 piece fresh ginger, very finely
　　chopped (1 inch long)
1 cinnamon stick (1 inch long)
1 teaspoon cumin seed *or* ¼
　　teaspoon ground cumin
1 bay leaf
3 medium tomatoes, chopped
½ teaspoon salt
½ teaspoon black pepper
⅛ teaspoon ground red pepper
2 tablespoons all-purpose flour
3 tablespoons water

Heat oil in large skillet or Dutch oven
over medium-high heat. Add onions,
garlic, cardamom pods, ginger,

Chicken Timatar

cinnamon stick, cumin seed and bay
leaf. Reduce heat to medium; cook and
stir 5 minutes. Add chicken, tomatoes,
salt, black pepper and ground red
pepper. Bring to a boil; reduce heat to
low. Cover tightly; simmer 30 minutes
or until chicken is tender and juices run
clear, turning after 15 minutes. Combine
flour and water; stir into tomato
mixture. Cook and stir 5 minutes or
until thickened. Remove and discard
cardamom pods, cinnamon stick and
bay leaf before serving.

Makes 6 servings

Favorite recipe from **Delmarva Poultry Industry, Inc.**

Saucy Chicken Breasts

2 tablespoons CRISCO® Shortening
1 pound boneless skinless chicken
　　breasts
2 large green onions with tops,
　　chopped (about ½ cup)
1 can (8¼ ounces) *or* 1 cup sliced
　　stewed tomatoes with juice
¼ cup dairy sour cream
½ teaspoon dried thyme leaves

1. Melt Crisco® in large, heavy skillet
over medium-high heat. Add chicken.
Cook 5 minutes on each side or until
chicken is tender and juices run clear.
Remove from skillet; set aside.

2. Reduce heat to medium. Add onions;
sauté about 3 minutes. Drain off any
excess Crisco®.

3. Stir in tomatoes with juice, sour
cream and thyme. Return chicken to
pan; spoon sauce over. Heat 5 minutes
longer or until heated through. *Do not
boil.* *Makes 4 servings*

Southwestern Oven-Fried Chicken

4 broiler-fryer chicken drumsticks,
   skinned (about 1 pound)
4 broiler-fryer chicken thighs,
   skinned (about 1 pound)
3 slices white bread, torn into small
   pieces
3 tablespoons fresh cilantro
2 tablespoons yellow cornmeal
2 tablespoons pine nuts
2 large cloves garlic, peeled
1½ teaspoons ground cumin
½ teaspoon dried oregano leaves,
   crumbled
½ teaspoon salt, divided
¼ teaspoon ground red pepper
⅛ teaspoon ground cloves
2 teaspoons slightly beaten egg
   white
2 tablespoons Dijon-style mustard
1 tablespoon water
2 teaspoons honey
¼ teaspoon black pepper

In blender or food processor container,
place bread, cilantro, cornmeal, pine
nuts, garlic, cumin, oregano, ¼
teaspoon salt, ground red pepper and
cloves. Process to form fine crumbs.
Add egg white; mix until moist. Place
mixture on large, shallow plate; set
aside.

In small bowl, mix together mustard,
water and honey; brush evenly over
chicken. Sprinkle chicken with black
pepper and remaining ¼ teaspoon salt.
Dip chicken, one piece at a time, in
bread crumb mixture, pressing gently so
thin coating adheres. Place chicken on
rack in greased jelly-roll pan. Bake in
400°F oven about 40 minutes or until
crisp and browned and fork can be
inserted into chicken with ease.

Makes 4 servings

Favorite recipe from **National Broiler Council**

Southwestern Oven-Fried Chicken

Chicken au Jardin

1 broiler-fryer chicken, cut up
   (2½ to 3½ pounds)
2 tablespoons butter or margarine
1 large onion, coarsely chopped
1 clove garlic, minced
1 can (10½ ounces) chicken broth
1 teaspoon salt
¾ teaspoon TABASCO® Pepper Sauce
½ teaspoon dried thyme leaves
1 cup chopped cooked ham or pork
2 cups sliced carrots
2 cups cut green beans
1 small zucchini, thinly sliced
3 medium tomatoes, peeled, diced
   Hot cooked rice or noodles

In large skillet over medium-high heat,
sauté chicken in butter until golden;
remove and reserve chicken. In
drippings, cook onion and garlic until
golden. Add broth, salt, Tabasco® sauce,
thyme, ham and reserved chicken.
Cover; simmer 20 minutes. Remove
chicken; set aside. Add vegetables;
arrange chicken on top. Boil 15 minutes
until chicken is tender and juices run
clear. Serve with rice.

Makes 4 to 6 servings

Chicken Mexicana

2 boneless skinless chicken breasts,
    halved (about 1¼ pounds)
¼ teaspoon garlic salt
2 tablespoons butter or margarine
½ cup sliced green onions with tops
    (½-inch slices)
½ cup chopped green bell pepper
2 to 3 cups hot cooked rice
1 cup PACE® Picante Sauce
4 ounces pasteurized process cheese
    spread, diced
    Additional PACE® Picante Sauce

Sprinkle chicken with garlic salt. Melt butter in large skillet over medium heat. Add chicken; cook 5 minutes. Turn chicken over; add green onions and green pepper around edge of skillet. Cook 5 minutes or until chicken is tender and juices run clear. Place rice on serving platter. Remove chicken and vegetables from skillet; arrange over rice. Keep warm.

Add 1 cup picante sauce and cheese spread to skillet. Cook and stir until cheese is melted and sauce is hot. Pour cheese sauce over chicken and vegetables. Garnish as desired. Serve with additional picante sauce.

Makes 4 servings

Brown Rice 'n' Broccoli Chicken

1 cup uncooked brown rice
2 tablespoons soy sauce
2 cups broccoli florets
2 cups cubed cooked chicken breast
1½ cups (6 ounces) shredded
    mozzarella cheese, divided
½ cup toasted sliced almonds*
¼ teaspoon pepper
¼ teaspoon garlic powder
    Dash ground nutmeg

Cook rice according to package directions, substituting soy sauce for 2 tablespoons of the water. Place broccoli florets in boiling salted water; boil 3 minutes. Rinse under cold water; drain well. Combine rice, broccoli, chicken, ½ cup of cheese, almonds, and seasonings in large bowl. Pour into buttered 13 × 9-inch baking dish or into individual buttered baking dishes. Sprinkle with remaining 1 cup cheese. Bake at 350°F for 20 to 25 minutes or until heated through.

Makes 6 servings

*See page 42 for directions for toasting almonds.

Favorite recipe from **USA Rice Council**

Chicken Mexicana

Ginger Spicy Chicken

Salt
2 boneless skinless chicken breasts,
  halved (about 1¼ pounds)
2 tablespoons vegetable oil
1 medium red bell pepper, cut into
  2 × ¼-inch strips
1 medium green bell pepper, cut
  into 2 × ¼-inch strips
1 can (8 ounces) pineapple chunks
  in juice, undrained
½ cup PACE® Picante Sauce
2 tablespoons chopped fresh cilantro
  or parsley
2 to 3 teaspoons grated fresh ginger
  or ¾ to 1 teaspoon ground
  ginger

Lightly salt chicken breasts. Heat oil in
large skillet over medium heat. Add
chicken; cook about 5 minutes on each
side or until light brown and tender.
Remove chicken; keep warm. Add
pepper strips, pineapple with juice,
picante sauce, cilantro and ginger to
skillet. Cook, stirring frequently, 5 to 7
minutes or until peppers are tender and
sauce is thickened. Return chicken to
skillet; heat through.

Makes 4 servings

Chicken with Savory Orzo

2 boneless skinless chicken breasts,
  halved (about 1¼ pounds)
2 tablespoons butter or margarine
1½ cups quartered mushrooms
1 cup chopped onion
½ teaspoon dried oregano leaves,
  crushed
½ teaspoon salt
⅛ teaspoon pepper
1 can (10¾ ounces) condensed
  chicken broth, undiluted
1 cup water
⅓ cup HEINZ® Chili Sauce
1 cup orzo (rice-shaped pasta)
2 tablespoons chopped pimiento
Chopped fresh parsley

Lightly flatten chicken breasts to
uniform thickness. In large skillet, sauté
chicken in butter until lightly browned
on both sides; remove. In same skillet,
add mushrooms, onion, oregano, salt
and pepper; sauté until onion is tender.
Stir in chicken broth, water and chili
sauce; bring to a boil. Stir in orzo and
pimiento. Cover; simmer 5 minutes.
Return chicken to skillet. Cover; simmer
an additional 10 minutes or until
chicken is tender and liquid is just
absorbed, stirring occasionally. Garnish
with parsley.

Makes 4 servings (about 3½ cups orzo)

Ginger Spicy Chicken

Microwaved Garlic and Herb Chicken

Microwaved Garlic and Herb Chicken

8 broiler-fryer chicken thighs (about 2 pounds)
½ **cup olive oil**
1 **large tomato, chopped**
1 **rib celery, sliced thin**
2 **tablespoons parsley flakes**
6 **cloves garlic, quartered**
1 **teaspoon salt**
½ **teaspoon pepper**
½ **teaspoon dried oregano leaves**
¼ **teaspoon dried basil leaves**
⅛ **teaspoon ground nutmeg**

Microwave Directions: In microwave-safe baking dish, mix together olive oil, tomato, celery, parsley, garlic, salt, pepper, oregano, basil and nutmeg. Microwave on HIGH 3 minutes; stir. Add chicken, covering with tomato mixture. Cover; refrigerate 3 hours or overnight. Cover baking dish with waxed paper; microwave on HIGH 10 minutes. Turn chicken over; cover again with waxed paper and microwave on HIGH 10 minutes. Let stand 5 minutes. If fork cannot be inserted into chicken with ease, return chicken to microwave for brief additional cooking at 1 minute intervals on HIGH. To serve, remove garlic quarters; spoon sauce over chicken. *Makes 4 servings*

Favorite recipe from **National Broiler Council**

Chili-Chicken Sombreros

2½ cups (13 ounces) cubed cooked
    chicken
  1 can (4 ounces) chopped green
    chilies, drained
1½ cups (6 ounces) shredded sharp
    Cheddar cheese
  1 medium tomato, chopped
  1 can (10¾ ounces) condensed cream
    of chicken soup
  ½ cup milk
  ½ teaspoon DURKEE® RedHot
    Cayenne Pepper Sauce (optional)
  ¾ cup biscuit baking mix
  ⅔ cup cornmeal
  ⅔ cup milk
  1 can (2.8 ounces) DURKEE® French
    Fried Onions
    DURKEE® Chili Powder

Preheat oven to 375°F. In greased 12 × 8-inch baking dish, layer chicken, chilies, *1 cup* cheese and tomato. In small bowl, combine soup, ½ cup milk and cayenne pepper sauce; pour evenly over chicken mixture. Bake, covered, 20 minutes.

Meanwhile, in medium bowl, combine baking mix, cornmeal, ⅔ cup milk and ½ *can* French Fried Onions; beat vigorously 30 seconds. Spoon biscuit dough in 8 mounds over top of casserole. Sprinkle biscuits with chili powder. Bake, uncovered, 20 minutes or until biscuits are light brown. Top biscuits with remaining cheese and onions; bake, uncovered, 3 minutes or until onions are golden brown.
Makes 6 to 8 servings

Grandma's Tomato Noodle Bake

  6 ounces wide noodles
  1 can (14½ ounces) DEL MONTE®
    Chunky Pasta Style Stewed
    Tomatoes, undrained
  ½ teaspoon dried basil leaves,
    crushed
  ¾ pound boneless skinless chicken
    breasts or thighs, cubed
  1 can (10¾ ounces) cream of celery
    soup, undiluted
  ⅓ cup sliced green onions
  1 cup (4 ounces) shredded Cheddar
    cheese
  1 cup crushed potato chips or French
    fried onion rings (optional)

Cook noodles according to package directions; drain. Drain tomatoes, reserving juice. In skillet, bring reserved juice and basil to a boil. Add chicken; cook until chicken is no longer pink in center, stirring frequently. Stir in tomatoes, soup, onions and noodles. In 2-quart baking dish, add noodle mixture; top with cheese and chips. Bake at 375°F, 15 minutes or until heated through.   *Makes 4 servings*

Prep and Cook Time: 25 minutes

THE CLASSICS

Here you'll find dazzling dishes with everlasting appeal. Chicken à l'Orange and Chicken Tetrazzini are just two of these popular palate pleasers.

Succulent Southern Fried Chicken

1 broiler-fryer chicken (about
   3 pounds)
2 tablespoons plus 2 teaspoons
   Chef Paul Prudhomme's
   POULTRY MAGIC®
2 cups all-purpose flour
2 large eggs, beaten well
2 cups milk
   Vegetable oil

Remove excess fat from chicken; cut into 8 pieces (cut breast in half). Season with Poultry Magic®, patting evenly to coat. Place in large, resealable plastic bag. Refrigerate overnight.

Remove chicken from refrigerator; let stand at room temperature 10 to 15 minutes. Measure flour into flat pan; reserve. Combine eggs with milk; reserve.

Pour oil to ¾-inch depth into large, heavy skillet; heat over high heat to 375°F. (This will take about 13 minutes.)

When oil is hot, and not before, coat half of chicken pieces with flour. Shake off excess; drop chicken pieces into egg mixture. Coat chicken pieces with flour again; shake off excess. Place chicken in single layer in hot oil (cook larger pieces first, skin side down). Adjust heat to maintain 340°F. Turn after about 8 minutes, or when chicken is golden brown. Cook about 5 minutes; turn again. (Second turning is to ensure crispiness and crunchiness.) Cook about 3 minutes; remove from skillet and drain on paper towels. Keep warm.

Reheat oil; repeat procedure for second batch. Garnish as desired.

Makes 6 servings

Succulent Southern Fried Chicken

Chicken-Rice Amandine

3/4 **pound boneless skinless chicken breasts, cut into strips**
1 **tablespoon vegetable oil**
2 **cups water**
1 **tablespoon cornstarch**
1/2 **package (16 ounces) BIRDS EYE® Farm Fresh Broccoli, Green Beans, Pearl Onions and Red Peppers (2 cups)**
1 **teaspoon salt**
1/4 **teaspoon black pepper**
1/4 **teaspoon dried tarragon leaves**
1 **chicken bouillon cube**
11/2 **cups MINUTE® Rice**
3 **tablespoons sliced almonds**

Cook and stir chicken in hot oil in large skillet until lightly browned. Mix water and cornstarch in bowl; stir into chicken. Add vegetables, seasonings and bouillon cube. Cook and stir until

Chicken-Rice Amandine

mixture thickens and comes to a full boil. Stir in rice. Cover; remove from heat. Let stand 5 minutes. Fluff with fork; sprinkle with almonds.

Makes 4 servings

Microwave Directions: Omit vegetable oil. Spread chicken in single layer in microwavable dish. Cover; microwave at HIGH 3 to 4 minutes. Mix water and cornstarch in bowl; stir into chicken. Add remaining ingredients except almonds. Cover; microwave at HIGH 3 minutes. Stir. Cover; microwave at HIGH 3 minutes. Stir again. Cover; microwave at HIGH 2 to 5 minutes. Let stand 5 minutes. Fluff with fork; sprinkle with almonds.

Chicken à l'Orange

2 **boneless skinless chicken breasts, halved (about 11/4 pounds)**
2 **tablespoons butter or margarine**
  Salt and pepper
2 **teaspoons cornstarch**
2/3 **cup orange juice**
1/3 **cup HEINZ® 57 Sauce**
1/4 **cup orange marmalade**
  Toasted slivered almonds*

Lightly flatten chicken breasts. In large skillet, sauté chicken in hot butter until tender and juices run clear, 8 to 10 minutes; season with salt and pepper to taste. Remove chicken; set aside. In small bowl, dissolve cornstarch in orange juice; stir in 57 Sauce and marmalade. Pour into skillet. Heat, stirring constantly, until mixture is hot and thickened. Return chicken to skillet; heat through. Spoon sauce over chicken; garnish with almonds.

Makes 4 servings (about 1 cup sauce)

*See page 42 for directions for toasting almonds.

Chicken Noodle Soup

5 (14½-ounce) cans ready-to-serve
    chicken broth
2 cups water
1 small onion, cut into small wedges
1 cup sliced carrots
1 cup sliced celery (including leaves)
2 tablespoons WYLER'S® or
    STEERO® Chicken-Flavor Instant
    Bouillon
1 teaspoon parsley flakes
1 teaspoon basil leaves
¼ teaspoon pepper
½ (1-pound) package CREAMETTE®
    Egg Noodles, uncooked
2 cups chopped cooked chicken

In Dutch oven, combine broth, water,
onion, carrots, celery, bouillon, parsley,
basil and pepper. Bring to boil. Reduce
heat; simmer 15 minutes. Prepare
noodles according to package directions;
drain. Add egg noodles and chicken to
soup; heat through. Garnish as desired.
Refrigerate leftovers.

Makes about 4 quarts soup

Oven-Barbecued Chicken

1 cup unsifted flour
1 teaspoon salt
3 pounds chicken pieces
¼ cup plus 2 tablespoons margarine
    or butter, melted
¼ cup chopped onion
1 clove garlic, finely chopped
1 cup ketchup
¼ cup firmly packed brown sugar
¼ cup REALEMON® Lemon Juice
    from Concentrate
¼ cup water
2 tablespoons Worcestershire sauce

Preheat oven to 350°F. In large plastic
bag, combine flour and salt. Add
chicken, a few pieces at a time; shake to
coat. Place in greased, 13 × 9-inch
baking dish; drizzle with ¼ *cup*
margarine. Bake, uncovered, 30
minutes.

Meanwhile, in small saucepan, cook
onion and garlic in remaining 2
tablespoons margarine until tender. Add
remaining ingredients; simmer,
uncovered, 10 minutes. Pour over
chicken; bake, uncovered, 30 minutes
longer or until tender. Refrigerate
leftovers.   *Makes 4 to 6 servings*

Quick 'n Easy Country Captain

3 tablespoons minced onion
1 clove garlic, minced
2 teaspoons curry powder
1 tablespoon butter or margarine
1½ cups chicken broth or bouillon
1½ cups UNCLE BEN'S® Rice In An
    Instant
1½ cups cubed cooked chicken
1 tomato, chopped
¼ cup raisins
⅓ cup salted peanuts (optional)

Cook onion, garlic and curry powder in
butter in medium saucepan 2 to 3
minutes. Add broth; bring to a boil. Stir
in rice, chicken, tomato and raisins.
Cover; remove from heat. Let stand 5
minutes or until all liquid is absorbed.
Sprinkle with peanuts, if desired.

Makes 4 servings

Stuffed Chicken Breasts

**4 boneless skinless chicken breast
    halves, pounded to ¼-inch
    thickness (about 1 pound)**
**½ teaspoon ground black pepper,
    divided**
¼ teaspoon salt
**1 cup cooked brown rice (cooked in
    chicken broth)**
¼ cup minced tomato
**¼ cup (1 ounce) finely shredded
    mozzarella cheese**
**3 tablespoons toasted rice bran*
    (optional)**
**1 tablespoon chopped fresh basil
    Vegetable cooking spray**

Season insides of chicken breasts with
¼ teaspoon pepper and salt. Combine
rice, tomato, cheese, bran, basil, and
remaining ¼ teaspoon pepper. Spoon
rice mixture on top of chicken; fold
chicken over and secure sides with
wooden toothpicks soaked in water.
Wipe off chicken with paper towel. Coat
a large skillet with cooking spray; place
over medium-high heat. Cook stuffed
chicken breasts 1 minute on each side
or just until golden brown. Transfer
stuffed chicken breasts to shallow
baking pan. Bake at 350°F for 8 to 10
minutes or until chicken is tender. Slice
to serve; garnish as desired.

Makes 4 servings

*To toast rice bran, spread on baking
sheet; bake at 325°F for 7 to 8 minutes.

*Favorite recipe from **USA Rice Council***

Old-Fashioned Chicken with Dumplings

3 to 3½ pounds chicken pieces
3 tablespoons butter or margarine
**2 cans (14½ ounces each) ready-to-
    serve chicken broth**
3½ cups water
1 teaspoon salt
¼ teaspoon white pepper
2 large carrots, cut into 1-inch slices
2 ribs celery, cut into 1-inch slices
8 to 10 small boiling onions
**¼ pound small mushrooms, cut into
    halves**
Parsley Dumplings (recipe follows)
½ cup frozen peas, thawed, drained

Brown chicken in melted butter in 6- to
8-quart saucepot over medium-high
heat. Add broth, water, salt and pepper.
Bring to a boil over high heat; reduce
heat to low. Cover; simmer 15 minutes.
Add carrots, celery, onions and
mushrooms. Cover; simmer 40 minutes
or until chicken and vegetables are
tender. Prepare Parsley Dumplings.

When chicken is tender, skim fat from
broth. Stir in peas. Drop dumpling
mixture onto chicken, making 6 large or
12 small dumplings. Cover; simmer 15
to 20 minutes or until dumplings are
firm to the touch and wooden toothpick
inserted in centers comes out clean.

Makes 6 servings

Parsley Dumplings: Sift 2 cups all-
purpose flour, 4 teaspoons baking
powder and ½ teaspoon salt into
medium bowl. Cut in 5 tablespoons
cold butter or margarine until mixture
resembles coarse meal. Make a well in
center; pour in 1 cup milk, all at once.
Add 2 tablespoons chopped fresh
parsley; stir with fork until dough
cleans sides of bowl. Makes 6 large or
12 small dumplings.

Stuffed Chicken Breast

Sweet 'n Sour Chicken

Sweet 'n Sour Chicken

1 pound boneless skinless chicken
    breasts, cut into cubes
2 tablespoons vegetable oil
1 cup green pepper strips
1 cup carrot strips
1 clove garlic, minced
1¼ cups chicken broth
1 can (8 ounces) pineapple chunks
    in juice, undrained
¼ cup soy sauce
3 tablespoons brown sugar
3 tablespoons vinegar
2 tablespoons dry sherry (optional)
½ teaspoon ground ginger
1½ cups MINUTE® Rice

Cook and stir chicken in hot oil in large
skillet until well browned. Add green
pepper, carrot and garlic; cook and stir
1 to 2 minutes.

Add broth, pineapple with juice, soy
sauce, brown sugar, vinegar, sherry and
ginger. Bring to a full boil. Stir in rice.
Cover; remove from heat. Let stand 5
minutes. Fluff with fork.

Makes 4 servings

Microwave Directions: Omit vegetable
oil and reduce broth to 1 cup. Mix
chicken, carrot and garlic in 2-quart
microwavable dish. Cover; microwave at
HIGH 3 minutes. Stir in remaining
ingredients. Cover; microwave at HIGH
5 to 6 minutes. Let stand 5 minutes.
Fluff with fork.

Coq au Vin

3 to 4 slices bacon, cut into ½-inch
    pieces
1 broiler-fryer chicken, cut up
    (2½ to 3 pounds)
1 envelope LIPTON® Beefy
    Mushroom Recipe Soup Mix
¼ teaspoon dried thyme leaves,
    crushed
1 clove garlic, minced
1½ cups dry red wine
½ cup water
2 cups frozen small whole onions
2 tablespoons chopped fresh parsley

Cook bacon in large skillet over
medium-high heat until crisp. Remove
from skillet with slotted spoon; drain
on paper towels. Brown chicken in
drippings; remove chicken and drain on
paper towels. Reserve drippings.

Stir beefy mushroom recipe soup mix,
thyme and garlic into reserved
drippings in skillet. Stir in wine and
water. Add chicken, bacon, onions and
parsley. Bring to a boil over high heat.
Reduce heat to low. Cover; simmer 45
minutes or until chicken is tender and
juices run clear, basting occasionally.

Makes 6 servings

Breast of Chicken Cordon Bleu

2 whole chicken breasts (about
    1 pound each), partially frozen
Salt
White pepper
1/2 cup milk
1 egg, slightly beaten
2 slices ham (1 1/2 ounces each)
2 thick slices Wisconsin Aged Swiss
    cheese (2 1/2 ounces each)
1/2 cup all-purpose flour
2 cups finely ground plain dry
    bread crumbs
1/2 cup (1 stick) butter

While chicken is ice cold, remove all bones from each whole breast. Do not sever skin at any point. (You may wish to have your butcher do this for you.) Sprinkle both sides of chicken with salt and pepper.

Combine milk and egg to make egg wash. Brush both sides of breasts completely with egg wash. Lay each whole breast, skin side down, on waxed paper. Place one slice each ham and cheese on half of each breast. Brush ham and cheese liberally with egg wash; fold chicken breast halves together, wrapping skin around all white meat.

Place flour, remaining egg wash and crumbs in three separate shallow dishes. Dip rolled chicken in flour, then in egg wash; roll in crumbs, packing crumbs to assure heavy, uniform coating. Wrap coated chicken in foil; refrigerate 6 hours or overnight.

Preheat oven to 350°F. Remove chicken from refrigerator. Melt butter in medium skillet over medium heat; brown chicken in butter. Remove chicken from skillet; reserve butter. Place chicken in baking pan. Pour reserved butter over chicken. Bake 35 to 40 minutes or until chicken is tender. When ready to serve, cut each chicken breast in half.

Makes 4 servings

*Favorite recipe from **Wisconsin Milk Marketing Board** © 1992*

Chicken-Asparagus Marsala

2 boneless skinless chicken breasts,
    halved (about 1 1/4 pounds)
2 tablespoons butter or margarine
1 tablespoon vegetable oil
1 package (10 ounces) frozen
    asparagus spears, partially
    thawed, cut diagonally into
    2-inch pieces
1/2 pound small mushrooms
1/4 cup Marsala wine
1/4 cup water
1/2 teaspoon salt
1/8 teaspoon pepper
1 tablespoon chopped fresh parsley

Pound chicken to 1/4-inch thickness. In skillet, heat butter and oil. Cook chicken about 5 minutes or until browned, turning once. Remove chicken; set aside. Add asparagus and mushrooms to pan drippings; cook 3 minutes, stirring constantly. Return chicken to pan; add wine, water, salt and pepper. Bring to a boil; boil 2 minutes. Reduce heat. Cover; simmer about 3 minutes or until chicken and vegetables are tender. Arrange chicken on platter; spoon vegetable sauce over chicken. Sprinkle with parsley. *Makes 4*

Makes 4 servings

*Favorite recipe from **Delmarva Poultry Industry, Inc.***

Chicken Diane

6 ounces uncooked pasta
³/₄ cup unsalted butter, divided
1 tablespoon plus 2 teaspoons
   Chef Paul Prudhomme's
   POULTRY MAGIC®
³/₄ pound boneless skinless chicken
   breasts, cut into strips
3 cups sliced mushrooms (about
   8 ounces)
¹/₄ cup minced green onion tops
3 tablespoons minced fresh parsley
1 teaspoon minced garlic
1 cup skimmed chicken stock or
   water

Cook pasta according to package directions to *al dente* stage. Drain immediately; rinse with hot water to wash off starch, then with cold water to stop cooking process. Drain again. To prevent pasta from sticking together, pour small amount of oil in palm of hand and rub through pasta.

Mash ¹/₄ cup butter in medium bowl; combine with Poultry Magic® and chicken. Heat large skillet over high heat until hot, about 4 minutes. Add chicken pieces and brown, about 2 minutes on one side and about 1 minute on the other. Add mushrooms; cook 2 minutes. Add green onion tops, parsley, garlic and stock. Cook 2 minutes or until sauce boils rapidly. Add remaining butter (cut into pats), stirring and shaking pan to incorporate. Cook 3 minutes; add hot cooked pasta. Stir and shake pan to mix well. Serve immediately. Garnish as desired.   *Makes 2 servings*

Chicken Livers in Wine Sauce

¹/₄ cup CRISCO® Oil
1 medium onion, cut into 8 pieces
¹/₂ cup chopped celery
¹/₄ cup snipped fresh parsley
1 clove garlic, minced
¹/₃ cup all-purpose flour
³/₄ teaspoon salt
¹/₄ teaspoon pepper
1 pound chicken livers, drained
¹/₂ cup water
¹/₂ cup milk
3 tablespoons dry white wine
³/₄ teaspoon instant chicken bouillon
   granules
¹/₂ teaspoon dried rosemary leaves
   Hot cooked egg noodles

1. Heat Crisco® Oil in large skillet. Add onion, celery, parsley and garlic. Sauté over medium heat until onion is tender. Set aside.

2. Mix flour, salt and pepper in large plastic bag. Add livers. Shake to coat. Add livers and any remaining flour mixture to onion mixture. Brown livers over medium-high heat, stirring occasionally. Stir in water, milk, wine, bouillon granules and rosemary. Heat to boiling, stirring constantly; reduce heat. Cover; simmer, stirring occasionally, 7 to 10 minutes, or until livers are no longer pink. Serve with noodles.
Makes 4 to 6 servings

Chicken Diane

Microwave Chicken Pot-au-Feu

2 boneless skinless chicken breasts, cut into 1-inch cubes (about 1¼ pounds)
1 large onion, coarsely chopped
3 cloves garlic, minced
1½ cups chicken broth
½ cup dry white wine
   TABASCO® Pepper Sauce
3 medium carrots, trimmed, peeled and cut into 2 × ¼-inch sticks
1 rib celery, sliced ½ inch thick
1 tablespoon cornstarch
1 cup peas (fresh, canned or frozen)
½ cup finely chopped fresh parsley *or* 2 teaspoons parsley flakes
1½ tablespoons fresh rosemary leaves *or* 1 teaspoon dried rosemary leaves
¼ teaspoon salt
¼ teaspoon black pepper

Microwave Directions: In 2-quart microwave-safe casserole, place chicken, onion, garlic, broth, wine, ½ teaspoon Tabasco® sauce, carrots and celery. Cover; microwave at HIGH 15 minutes or until chicken is no longer pink in center and vegetables are tender, stirring once. Uncover. Dissolve cornstarch in ¼ cup cooking liquid. Add to chicken mixture; stir thoroughly until blended. Add peas, parsley and rosemary. Cover; microwave at HIGH 3 minutes or until sauce has thickened. Season with salt, pepper and additional Tabasco® sauce. *Makes 4 servings*

Microwave Chicken Pot-au-Feu

Chicken Breasts Fricassee

2 small boneless skinless chicken
   breasts, halved (about
   1¼ pounds)
¼ cup all-purpose flour
¼ teaspoon salt
   Dash pepper
2 tablespoons olive or vegetable oil
1 tablespoon butter or margarine
1 clove garlic, finely chopped
1 cup sliced mushrooms
½ cup chopped onion
¼ cup dry white wine
2 cups water
1 package LIPTON® Rice & Sauce –
   Chicken Flavor
½ cup frozen peas, thawed
   Chopped fresh parsley for garnish

Dip chicken in flour combined with salt and pepper. In large skillet, heat oil; cook chicken over medium heat 5 minutes or until chicken is tender and juices run clear. Remove to serving platter; keep warm.

Into skillet, add butter, garlic, mushrooms and onion; cook over medium heat, stirring occasionally, 3 minutes or until mushrooms are tender. Add wine; boil 30 seconds. Add water; bring to a boil. Stir in rice & chicken flavor sauce. Simmer, stirring occasionally, 10 minutes or until rice is tender. Stir in peas. Garnish with parsley. Serve rice with chicken.

Makes 4 servings

Chicken Kiev

4 boneless skinless chicken breasts,
   halved (about 2½ pounds)
1 teaspoon salt
⅓ cup butter or margarine, softened
1 tablespoon minced fresh parsley
1 teaspoon lemon juice
1 clove garlic, minced
1½ cups plain dry bread crumbs
⅓ cup all-purpose flour
2 eggs, slightly beaten
   CRISCO® Shortening
   Hot cooked brown rice

1. Sprinkle chicken with salt.

2. Cream butter, parsley, lemon juice and garlic. Spread 2 teaspoons butter mixture in the center of each chicken breast half. Tuck ends and long sides around butter mixture; roll and skewer or tie to close.

3. Place crumbs, flour and eggs into separate shallow dishes. Dip each prepared chicken breast into flour, then eggs; roll in crumbs to coat evenly. Place, seam side down, on plate; cover and refrigerate at least 2 hours or until crumbs are set.

4. Heat 1½-inch layer of Crisco® to 365°F in deep saucepan or deep fryer. Fry chicken rolls in hot Crisco® 5 minutes or until tender. Remove with slotted spoon. Serve immediately with brown rice.

Makes 8 servings

Chicken Divan

2 packages (10 ounces each) frozen
   broccoli spears
¼ cup CRISCO® Shortening
¼ cup all-purpose flour
½ teaspoon salt
1 cup chicken broth
¼ cup crumbled blue cheese
1 cup whipping cream
3 boneless skinless chicken breasts,
   cooked and sliced (about
   2 pounds)
¾ cup grated Parmesan cheese,
   divided

1. Preheat oven to 375°F. Grease
6 broiler-proof 10-ounce or larger
individual baking dishes (ramekins).

2. Cook broccoli in unsalted boiling
water in large saucepan just until
tender; drain.

3. Melt Crisco® in small saucepan over
medium-high heat. Blend in flour and
salt; cook until mixture bubbles, stirring
constantly. Gradually stir in chicken
broth. Continue cooking and stirring
until sauce comes to a boil and is
thickened. Remove from heat. Add blue
cheese; stir until melted. Blend in cream
with wire whisk.

4. Divide cooked broccoli among baking
dishes. Spoon about ¼ cup sauce over
each serving. Place chicken over sauce.

5. Stir half of Parmesan cheese (about
6 tablespoons) into remaining sauce.
Spoon sauce equally over chicken.
Sprinkle each serving with 1 tablespoon
remaining Parmesan cheese.

6. Bake at 375°F for 15 minutes or until
bubbly and lightly browned. Place
broiler rack so that tops of baking
dishes are about 5 inches from heat.

Turn temperature control to broil. Broil 1 to
2 minutes. (If baking dishes are not
broiler-proof, eliminate this last broiling
step.) *Makes 6 servings*

Chicken and Rice Paprikash

1 tablespoon paprika, divided
¾ teaspoon salt
¼ teaspoon black pepper
6 medium chicken thighs (2½ to
   3 pounds)
1 can (14½ or 16 ounces) whole
   tomatoes, undrained
1 teaspoon chicken bouillon
   granules
1 small onion, sliced and separated
   into rings
2 cloves garlic, minced
1 cup UNCLE BEN'S®
   CONVERTED® Brand Rice
1 large green bell pepper, cut into
   thin strips
   Light sour cream or plain yogurt
   (optional)

Combine 1½ teaspoons paprika, salt
and black pepper. Rub seasonings onto
chicken thighs, coating all surfaces; set
aside. Drain tomatoes, reserving juice.
Chop tomatoes; set aside. Add enough
water to reserved juice to equal 2 cups.
Combine tomato liquid, bouillon
granules, onion, garlic and remaining
1½ teaspoons paprika in 12-inch skillet.
Bring to a boil. Stir in rice and
tomatoes. Arrange chicken thighs on
top of rice mixture. Cover tightly;
simmer 20 minutes. Add green pepper.
Remove from heat. Let stand, covered,
until all liquid is absorbed and chicken
is tender, about 5 minutes. Serve with
sour cream. *Makes 6 servings*

Forty-Clove Chicken Filice

Forty-Clove Chicken Filice

1 broiler-fryer chicken, cut up
    (about 3 pounds)
40 cloves fresh garlic, peeled and
    left whole
$\frac{1}{2}$ cup dry white wine
$\frac{1}{4}$ cup dry vermouth
$\frac{1}{4}$ cup olive oil
4 ribs celery, thickly sliced
2 tablespoons finely chopped fresh
    parsley
2 teaspoons dried basil leaves
1 teaspoon dried oregano leaves
    Pinch crushed red pepper flakes
1 lemon
    Salt and black pepper

Preheat oven to 375°F. Place chicken pieces, skin side up, in single layer in shallow baking pan. Combine garlic, wine, vermouth, oil, celery, parsley, basil, oregano and red pepper in medium bowl; mix thoroughly. Sprinkle garlic mixture over chicken pieces. Remove zest* from lemon in thin strips; place zest throughout pan. Squeeze juice from lemon; pour over top. Season with salt and black pepper. Cover pan with aluminum foil. Bake 40 minutes. Remove foil; bake 15 minutes. Garnish as desired.

Makes 4 to 6 servings

*See page 48 for information about zest.

Favorite recipe from **The Fresh Garlic Association**

Louisiana Tomato-Rice Gumbo

1 boneless chicken breast, cut up
  (about 10 ounces)
3 tablespoons butter or margarine
$1/2$ cup chopped onion
$1/2$ cup chopped green pepper
$1/2$ cup chopped celery
1 clove garlic, minced
1 package (10 ounces) frozen okra,
  thawed and sliced*
1 can (16 ounces) crushed tomatoes
1 can ($13^3/4$ ounces) ready-to-serve
  chicken broth
1 teaspoon salt
1 small bay leaf
$1/2$ teaspoon sugar
$1/8$ teaspoon dried thyme leaves
  Dash of black pepper
$1/2$ pound shrimp, cleaned
$1^1/3$ cups MINUTE® Rice

Cook and stir chicken in hot butter in large skillet until lightly browned. Stir in onion, green pepper, celery and garlic; cook until chicken and vegetables are tender.

Add okra, tomatoes, broth and seasonings. Bring to a boil; reduce heat. Cover; simmer 5 minutes, stirring occasionally. Add shrimp; cook 5 minutes. Remove and discard bay leaf. Stir in rice. Cover; remove from heat. Let stand 5 minutes.

Makes 6 servings

*Substitute 1 package (10 ounces) Birds Eye® Cut Green Beans, thawed, for the frozen okra.

Chicken Tetrazzini

8 ounces uncooked spaghetti,
  broken in half
3 tablespoons butter, divided
$1/4$ cup all-purpose flour
1 teaspoon salt
$1/2$ teaspoon paprika
$1/2$ teaspoon celery salt
$1/8$ teaspoon pepper
2 cups milk
1 cup chicken broth
3 cups chopped cooked chicken
1 can (4 ounces) mushrooms,
  drained
$1/4$ cup pimiento strips
$3/4$ cup grated Wisconsin Parmesan
  cheese, divided

In large saucepan, cook spaghetti according to package directions; drain. Return to same saucepan; add 1 tablespoon butter. Stir until melted. Set aside. In 3-quart saucepan, melt remaining 2 tablespoons butter over medium heat; stir in flour, salt, paprika, celery salt and pepper. Remove from heat; gradually stir in milk and chicken broth. Cook over medium heat, stirring constantly, until thickened. Add chicken, mushrooms, pimiento, spaghetti and $1/4$ cup cheese; heat thoroughly. Place chicken mixture on ovenproof platter or in shallow casserole; sprinkle remaining $1/2$ cup cheese over top. Broil about 3 inches from heat until lightly browned.

Makes 6 to 8 servings

*Favorite recipe from **Wisconsin Milk Marketing Board** © 1992*

Louisiana Tomato-Rice Gumbo

Dijon Chicken Elegant

4 boneless chicken breasts, halved
    (about 2½ pounds)
⅓ cup GREY POUPON® Dijon or
    Country Dijon Mustard
1 teaspoon dried dill weed *or*
    1 tablespoon chopped fresh dill
8 slices Swiss cheese (4 ounces)
2 frozen puff pastry sheets, thawed
1 egg white
1 tablespoon cold water

Pound chicken to ½-inch thickness.
Blend mustard and dill; spread on
chicken. Top each chicken breast half
with cheese slice; roll up.

Roll each pastry sheet into 12-inch
square; cut each square into four 6-inch
squares. Beat egg white and water;
brush edges of each square with egg
mixture. Place one chicken roll
diagonally on each square. Join four
points of pastry over chicken; press to
seal seams. Place on ungreased baking
sheet. Brush with remaining egg
mixture. Bake at 375°F, 30 minutes or
until pastry is golden brown. Serve
immediately.   *Makes 8 servings*

Basic Chicken Stock

1 broiler-fryer chicken, cut up (3 to
    4 pounds)
1 small onion, cut into quarters
1 clove garlic, cut in half
1 bay leaf
3 parsley sprigs
½ teaspoon salt
⅛ teaspoon black peppercorns
4 cups water

Place chicken in 5-quart Dutch oven.
Add remaining ingredients. Bring to a
boil; reduce heat. Cover; simmer 45
minutes or until meat near thigh bone
is no longer pink.

Transfer chicken to plate with slotted
spoon; let cool. Strain stock; discard
solids.

Remove chicken from bones; discard
skin and bones. Shred chicken; save for
another use.   *Makes about 3 cups stock*

Storing Basic Chicken Stock
Refrigerate stock up to 2 days, removing
top fat layer only just before using stock
for best results.

Freeze defatted stock up to 6 months,
storing in well-sealing plastic containers.

Special Lemony Chicken

¼ cup unsifted flour
1 teaspoon salt
¼ teaspoon pepper
6 skinned boneless chicken breast
    halves (about 1½ pounds)
¼ cup margarine or butter
¼ cup REALEMON® Lemon Juice
    from Concentrate
8 ounces fresh mushrooms, sliced
    (about 2 cups)
Hot cooked rice
Chopped fresh parsley

In large plastic bag, combine flour, salt
and pepper. Add chicken, a few pieces
at a time; shake to coat. In large skillet,
brown chicken in margarine. Add
ReaLemon® brand and mushrooms.
Reduce heat; cover and simmer 15
minutes or until tender. Serve with rice;
garnish with parsley. Refrigerate
leftovers.   *Makes 6 servings*

Chicken Florentine

¾ pound boneless skinless chicken
   breasts, cut into strips
1 small onion, chopped
2 tablespoons butter or margarine
1 clove garlic, minced
1 package (10 ounces) BIRDS EYE®
   Chopped Spinach
1 cup chicken broth
½ cup water
1 cup MINUTE® Rice
⅓ cup grated Parmesan cheese

Cook and stir chicken and onion in hot
butter in large skillet until chicken is
lightly browned. Add garlic; cook 30
seconds. Add spinach, broth and water.
Bring to a boil. Reduce heat; simmer 3
minutes. Stir in rice and cheese. Cover;
remove from heat. Let stand 5 minutes.
Fluff with fork. *Makes 3 servings*

Microwave Directions: Thaw and drain
spinach, reduce broth to ¾ cup and
omit butter. Mix together chicken, onion
and garlic in microwavable dish. Cover;
microwave at HIGH 3 minutes. Stir in
spinach, broth, water and rice. Cover;
microwave at HIGH 6 minutes. Let
stand 5 minutes. Fluff with fork. Stir in
cheese.

Honey-Roasted Chicken

1 broiler-fryer chicken (about
   2½ pounds)
½ cup water
¼ cup honey
2 tablespoons olive oil
½ teaspoon curry powder
1 teaspoon salt
½ teaspoon pepper
1 can (16 ounces) peach halves,
   drained

Honey-Roasted Chicken

Pour water into bottom of 13 × 9-inch
baking pan with roasting rack. In small
saucepan, mix together honey, oil and
curry powder; bring to a boil over
medium heat.* Place chicken on rack,
breast side up; brush with honey
mixture. Spoon 2 teaspoons of mixture
into center cavity; season chicken with
salt and pepper. Roast chicken in 375°F
oven 30 minutes. Remove from oven.
Turn chicken over; arrange peach halves
in bottom of pan. Spoon pan juices over
chicken and peaches; return to oven.
Roast 30 minutes or until fork can be
inserted into chicken with ease. Garnish
as desired. *Makes 4 servings*

*Honey mixture can be microwaved
in glass measuring cup at HIGH for
2 minutes.

*Favorite recipe from **National Broiler Council***

Brunswick Stew

1 stewing chicken, cut into serving
    pieces (about 4½ pounds)
2 quarts water
1 rib celery (including leaves), cut
    into 2-inch pieces
1 small onion, quartered
1 small clove garlic, halved
2 teaspoons salt
1 teaspoon whole peppercorns
1 can (16 ounces) tomatoes, cut into
    1-inch pieces
¼ cup tomato paste
2 medium potatoes, pared and
    cubed
1 onion, thinly sliced
1 teaspoon sugar
½ teaspoon ground pepper
½ teaspoon dried thyme leaves
⅛ teaspoon garlic powder
    Dash red pepper sauce
1 package (10 ounces) frozen lima
    beans
1 package (10 ounces) frozen whole
    kernel corn

Place chicken, giblets and neck in
5-quart Dutch oven; add water. Heat to
boiling; skim off foam. Add celery,
quartered onion, garlic, salt and
peppercorns; heat to boiling. Reduce
heat. Cover; simmer until thighs are
tender, 2½ to 3 hours.

Remove chicken pieces from broth; cool
slightly. Remove meat from chicken,
discarding bones and skin. Cut enough
chicken into 1-inch pieces to measure 3
cups. (Reserve remaining chicken for
another use.)

Strain broth through double thickness
of cheesecloth, discarding vegetables;
skim off fat. Return 1 quart broth to
Dutch oven. (Reserve remaining broth
for another use.) Add tomatoes, tomato
paste, potatoes, sliced onion, sugar,
ground pepper, thyme, garlic powder
and red pepper sauce. Cook until
boiling; reduce heat. Cover; simmer 30
minutes.

Add beans and corn to stew. Cook until
stew boils. Reduce heat. Cover; cook 5
minutes. Add chicken pieces; cook 5
minutes. Serve hot.

Makes 6 to 8 servings

Chicken à la King

1 pound boneless skinless chicken
    breasts, cut into strips
2 tablespoons butter or margarine
1 jar (12 ounces) home-style chicken
    gravy
1 package (10 ounces) BIRDS EYE®
    Green Peas
1 cup milk
1 jar (4½ ounces) sliced mushrooms,
    drained
2 tablespoons dry sherry (optional)
½ teaspoon salt
⅛ teaspoon pepper
1½ cups MINUTE® Rice
1 jar (4 ounces) pimiento pieces

Cook and stir chicken in hot butter in
large skillet until lightly browned. Add
gravy, peas, milk, mushrooms, sherry,
salt and pepper. Bring to a boil; reduce
heat. Cover; simmer 2 minutes. Return
to a full boil. Stir in rice and pimiento.
Cover; remove from heat. Let stand 5
minutes. Fluff with fork.

Makes 4 servings

Brunswick Stew

Creamy Chicken Tarragon

2 tablespoons vegetable oil
1 broiler-fryer chicken, cut up
   (2½ to 3 pounds)
1 envelope LIPTON® Onion, Onion-
   Mushroom or Golden Onion
   Recipe Soup Mix
½ teaspoon dried tarragon leaves
1 cup water
½ cup dry white wine
2 tablespoons all-purpose flour
½ cup whipping cream

In large skillet, heat oil over medium heat and brown chicken; drain. Add onion recipe soup mix and tarragon blended with water and wine. Simmer, covered, 45 minutes or until chicken is tender. Remove chicken to serving platter; keep warm.

Into skillet, stir in flour blended with cream. Bring to a boil; simmer, stirring constantly, until sauce is thickened, about 5 minutes. Serve sauce over chicken.   *Makes 4 servings*

Microwave Directions: Omit vegetable oil. In 3-quart microwave-safe dish, microwave chicken, uncovered, at HIGH 12 minutes, rearranging once; drain. Add onion recipe soup mix and tarragon blended with water and wine. Microwave, covered, at HIGH 14 minutes or until chicken is tender, rearranging chicken once. Remove chicken to serving platter; keep warm. Into dish, stir in flour blended with cream; microwave, uncovered, at HIGH 4 minutes or until sauce is thickened, stirring once. Serve as directed.

Chicken Pot Pie

1 can (10¾ ounces) cream of chicken
   soup
1 cup milk, divided
½ cup chopped onion
1 package (3 ounces) cream cheese,
   softened and cut up
¼ cup chopped celery
¼ cup shredded carrot
¼ cup grated Wisconsin Parmesan
   cheese
3 cups cubed cooked chicken
1 package (10 ounces) frozen cut
   broccoli, cooked and drained
1 cup packaged complete buttermilk
   pancake mix
1 cup (4 ounces) shredded
   Wisconsin Sharp Cheddar cheese
1 egg, slightly beaten
1 tablespoon vegetable oil
¼ cup sliced almonds

In large saucepan, combine soup, ½ cup milk, onion, cream cheese, celery, carrot and Parmesan cheese. Cook and stir over medium–high heat until mixture is hot and cream cheese is melted. Stir in chicken and broccoli; heat through. Pour into ungreased 2-quart casserole.

For topping, in medium mixing bowl, combine pancake mix and Cheddar cheese. In small mixing bowl, stir together egg, remaining ½ cup milk and oil. Add to pancake mixture; stir until well combined. Spoon topping over hot chicken mixture. Sprinkle with nuts. Bake at 375°F, 20 to 25 minutes or until topping is golden brown and chicken mixture is bubbly around the edges.   *Makes 6 to 8 servings*

Prep Time: 45 minutes

Favorite recipe from Wisconsin Milk Marketing Board © 1992

Cobb Salad

2 boneless skinless chicken breasts,
halved, cooked and cooled
(about 1¼ pounds)
⅔ cup vegetable oil
⅓ cup HEINZ® Distilled White or
Apple Cider Vinegar
1 clove garlic, minced
2 teaspoons dried dill weed
1½ teaspoons sugar
½ teaspoon salt
¼ teaspoon black pepper
8 cups torn salad greens, chilled
1 large tomato, diced
1 medium green bell pepper, diced
1 small red onion, chopped
¾ cup crumbled blue cheese
6 slices bacon, cooked, crumbled
1 hard-cooked egg, chopped

Shred chicken into bite-size pieces. For
dressing, in jar, combine oil, vinegar,
garlic, dill, sugar, salt and black pepper;
cover and shake vigorously. Pour ½ cup
dressing over chicken; toss well to coat.
Toss greens with remaining dressing.
Line each of 4 large individual salad
plates with greens; mound chicken
mixture on plates. Arrange mounds of
tomato, green pepper, onion, cheese,
bacon and egg around chicken mixture.

Makes 4 servings

Cobb Salad

Chicken, Andouille Smoked Sausage and Tasso Jambalaya

3 tablespoons unsalted butter
½ pound andouille smoked sausage*
  (preferred) or any other good
  smoked pure pork sausage, such
  as Polish sausage (kielbasa), cut
  into ¼-inch slices
½ pound tasso** (preferred) or other
  lean smoked ham, diced
¾ pound boneless skinless chicken
  breasts, cut into bite-size pieces
  (about 2 cups)
2 bay leaves
2 tablespoons plus ¾ teaspoon
  Chef Paul Prudhomme's
  POULTRY MAGIC®
1 cup chopped onion, divided
1 cup chopped celery, divided
1 cup chopped green bell pepper,
  divided
1 tablespoon minced garlic
½ cup tomato sauce
1 cup peeled, chopped tomatoes
2½ cups skimmed chicken stock or
  water
1½ cups uncooked rice (preferably
  converted)

Melt butter in 4-quart saucepan over high heat. Add andouille and tasso; cook until meat starts to brown, 4 to 5 minutes, stirring frequently and scraping pan bottom well. Add chicken; cook until chicken is browned, 4 to 5 minutes, stirring frequently and scraping pan bottom well.

Stir in bay leaves, Poultry Magic®, ½ cup onion, ½ cup celery, ½ cup bell pepper and garlic. Cook until vegetables start to soften, 6 to 8 minutes, stirring frequently and scraping pan bottom well. Stir in tomato sauce; cook about 1 minute, stirring frequently. Stir in remaining onion, celery, bell pepper and tomatoes.

Stir in stock and rice, mixing well. Bring mixture to a boil, stirring occasionally. Reduce heat. Cover; simmer over very low heat until rice is tender, but still chewy, about 30 minutes. (Or, after stock and rice are added, transfer mixture to an ungreased 13 × 9-inch baking pan and bake, uncovered, at 350°F until rice is tender, but still chewy, about 1 hour.)

Stir well; remove and discard bay leaves. Let stand, uncovered, 5 minutes before serving. Arrange 2 heaping mounds of jambalaya on each serving plate. *Makes 6 servings*

*Andouille smoked sausage is a spicy smoked sausage that is common to Cajun cooking; it can be found in gourmet and specialty food shops and some butcher shops.

**Tasso is lean, cured pork, heavily spiced with seasonings, that is common to Cajun cooking; it can be found in gourmet and specialty food shops and some butcher shops.

Chicken, Andouille Smoked Sausage and Tasso Jambalaya

Classic Chicken Curry with Winter Fruit and Walnuts

4 tablespoons butter
2 cloves garlic, minced
1 tablespoon curry powder
1 teaspoon paprika
1/4 teaspoon ground red pepper
    (optional)
1 tablespoon cornstarch
1 cup chicken broth
3 boneless skinless chicken breasts,
    halved (about 2 pounds)
2 pears, cored and thickly sliced
3/4 cup chopped California walnuts
1/2 cup chopped green onions
1/4 cup cranberries or currants
    Hot cooked rice or couscous
    (optional)

Microwave Directions: Microwave butter in uncovered 3-quart glass casserole dish 2 minutes on HIGH. Stir in garlic and spices; microwave on HIGH 3 minutes. Mix cornstarch with broth and add to garlic mixture; stir. Arrange chicken in single layer in sauce. Cover; microwave on HIGH 6 to 8 minutes, stirring every 2 minutes. Stir in pears, walnuts, green onions and cranberries. Cover; microwave on HIGH an additional 6 to 8 minutes or until chicken is tender and no longer pink in center. Arrange chicken and pears on serving platter. Pour remaining sauce over chicken; serve with rice.

Makes 4 to 6 servings

Favorite recipe from **Walnut Marketing Board**

Chicken Cacciatore

1/3 cup all-purpose flour
1 broiler-fryer chicken, cut up
    (2 1/2 to 3 pounds)
1/4 cup CRISCO® Oil
1 medium onion, thinly sliced and
    separated into rings
1/2 cup chopped green bell pepper
2 cloves garlic, minced
1 can (14 1/2 ounces) whole tomatoes,
    undrained
1 can (8 ounces) tomato sauce
1 can (4 ounces) sliced mushrooms,
    drained
3/4 teaspoon salt
1/2 teaspoon dried oregano leaves
    Hot cooked noodles

1. Place flour in large plastic bag. Add a few chicken pieces. Shake to coat. Remove chicken from bag. Repeat with remaining chicken.

2. Heat Crisco® Oil in large skillet. Add chicken. Brown over medium-high heat. Remove chicken from skillet; set aside.

3. Add onion, green pepper and garlic to skillet. Sauté over medium heat until tender. Add tomatoes, tomato sauce, mushrooms, salt and oregano, stirring to break apart tomatoes.

4. Place chicken pieces on top of tomato mixture. Reduce heat. Cover; simmer 30 to 40 minutes, or until chicken is tender and meat near bone is no longer pink. Serve with noodles.   *Makes 4 servings*

Poulet Provençale

Poulet Provençale

2 to 3 pounds chicken pieces
3 tablespoons olive or vegetable oil
1 medium onion, coarsely chopped
1 tablespoon all-purpose flour
1 can (28 ounces) whole tomatoes,
  cut up
1 teaspoon dried oregano leaves,
  crushed
1 teaspoon dried basil leaves,
  crushed
1 teaspoon LAWRY'S® Seasoned Salt
3/4 teaspoon LAWRY'S® Garlic Powder
  with Parsley
1/4 teaspoon LAWRY'S® Seasoned
  Pepper

In heavy Dutch oven over medium-high heat, brown chicken in hot oil until golden; remove and set aside. Add onion; sauté 1 to 2 minutes. Drain fat. Return chicken to Dutch oven; sprinkle with flour.

In medium bowl, combine remaining ingredients; blend well. Add to chicken. Bring to a boil; reduce heat. Cover; simmer 35 to 45 minutes or until chicken is tender. Transfer chicken to serving platter. Cook sauce over medium-high heat until reduced to desired consistency; pour over chicken.

Makes 4 to 6 servings

Presentation: Serve in deep-rimmed plates with fresh green beans or whipped potatoes and sweet rolls.

ETHNIC FLAVORS

Savor these international flavors! Beijing Chicken, Arroz con Pollo and Chicken & Pasta Sicilian come sprinkled with foreign intrigue.

Chicken Chow Mein

1 pound boneless skinless chicken breasts or thighs
2 cloves garlic, minced
2 tablespoons peanut or vegetable oil, divided
¼ cup soy sauce
2 tablespoons dry sherry
2 cups (6 ounces) fresh snow peas *or* 1 package (6 ounces) frozen snow peas, thawed, cut into halves
3 large green onions, cut diagonally into 1-inch pieces
6 ounces uncooked Chinese egg noodles or vermicelli, cooked, drained and rinsed
1 tablespoon sesame oil

Cut chicken into ¼-inch slices; cut each slice into 1×¼-inch strips. Toss chicken with garlic in small bowl.

Heat wok or large skillet over medium-high heat. Add 1 tablespoon peanut oil; heat until hot. Add chicken mixture; stir-fry 3 minutes or until chicken is no longer pink in center. Transfer chicken mixture to bowl; toss with soy sauce and sherry.

Heat remaining 1 tablespoon peanut oil in wok. Add snow peas; stir-fry 2 minutes for fresh or 1 minute for frozen snow peas. Add onions; stir-fry 30 seconds. Add chicken mixture; stir-fry 1 minute.

Add noodles to wok; stir-fry 2 minutes or until heated through. Stir in sesame oil; serve immediately.

Makes 4 servings

Chicken Chow Mein

Scandinavian Chicken

Scandinavian Chicken

6 boneless skinless chicken thighs,
   cut into 1-inch pieces
3 tablespoons butter
1 teaspoon salt
1/4 teaspoon pepper
2/3 cup finely chopped onion
8 ounces mushrooms, sliced
3/4 cup sour cream
1/2 cup (2 ounces) shredded Havarti
   cheese
1/4 cup plain fresh bread crumbs
2 tablespoons chopped fresh parsley

In skillet, melt butter over medium-high
heat. Add chicken; cook, stirring often,
about 7 minutes or until browned on all
sides. Sprinkle with salt and pepper.
Add onion; cook and stir until onion is
clear, about 5 minutes. Add
mushrooms; cook 5 minutes more,
stirring occasionally, until fork can be
inserted into chicken with ease. Reduce
heat to low; stir in sour cream and
cheese. Cook until cheese melts, about
2 minutes. Stir in crumbs; sprinkle with
parsley.   *Makes 4 servings*

Favorite recipe from **National Broiler Council**

Arroz con Pollo

6 pounds chicken pieces
1/4 cup FILIPPO BERIO® Olive Oil
2 cups uncooked long-grain rice
1 large onion, cut lengthwise into
   halves, then sliced crosswise
2 large cloves garlic, minced
3 cups chicken broth
1 can (14 1/2 ounces) tomatoes, cut up,
   undrained
1 teaspoon salt
1/2 teaspoon dried oregano leaves,
   crushed
1/4 teaspoon pepper
1/4 teaspoon dried saffron threads,
   crushed
1 1/2 cups sliced pepperoni
1 package (10 ounces) frozen peas
1 cup pimiento strips
1/2 cup pimiento-stuffed green olive
   halves

Brown chicken, a few pieces at a time,
in hot oil in large skillet over medium-
high heat until golden. Remove chicken
as it browns; drain on paper towels.
Add rice, onion and garlic to skillet.
Cook until rice is golden, stirring
frequently. Combine rice mixture, broth,
tomatoes, salt, oregano, pepper and
saffron in 13×9-inch baking dish. Top
with pepperoni and chicken. Cover
with foil. Bake at 350°F, 1 hour.
Uncover; add peas, pimiento and olives.
Bake, uncovered, 10 minutes or until
chicken is tender and juices run clear.
                    Makes 8 to 10 servings

Pollo alla Firènze

3 boneless chicken breasts, halved
   (about 2 pounds)
2 cups plus 2 tablespoons dry sherry
3 tablespoons olive oil
3 cups fresh spinach leaves,
   shredded
2 cups coarsely chopped mushrooms
1 cup grated carrots
1/3 cup sliced green onions
2 cloves garlic, minced
   Salt and pepper
1 cup Italian seasoned dry bread
   crumbs
1/4 cup grated Romano cheese
1 1/2 cups prepared Italian salad
   dressing

Place chicken in large, shallow dish;
add 2 cups sherry. Cover; marinate in
refrigerator at least 3 hours.

Heat oil in large skillet over medium heat. Add spinach, mushrooms, carrots, onions, garlic, salt and pepper to taste and remaining 2 tablespoons sherry. Cook and stir 3 to 5 minutes or until spinach is completely wilted; cool. Combine bread crumbs with 1/4 cup Romano cheese in shallow dish; set aside. Place dressing in another shallow dish; set aside.

Preheat oven to 375°F. Remove chicken from marinade; discard marinade. Slice a pocket into side of each chicken breast; fill with spinach mixture. Secure with wooden toothpicks, if necessary. Dip each filled breast into dressing, then place in bread crumb mixture. Spoon bread crumb mixture over chicken to cover completely. Place chicken in single layer in greased 13×9-inch baking pan. Drizzle with remaining dressing. Cover; bake 15 minutes. Uncover; bake 10 to 15 minutes or until chicken is tender and juices run clear. *Makes 6 servings*

Pollo alla Firènze

Rio Grande Quesadillas

2 cups shredded cooked chicken
1 package (1.25 ounces) LAWRY'S®
Taco Spices & Seasonings
³/₄ cup water
1 can (16 ounces) refried beans
6 large flour tortillas
1¹/₂ cups (6 ounces) shredded
Monterey Jack cheese
¹/₄ cup chopped pimiento
¹/₄ cup chopped green onions
¹/₄ cup chopped fresh cilantro
Vegetable oil

In medium skillet, combine chicken, Taco Spices & Seasonings and water. Bring to a boil; reduce heat and simmer, uncovered, 15 minutes. Stir in refried beans. On half of each tortilla, spread approximately ¹/₃ cup chicken-bean mixture. Top each with equal portions of cheese, pimiento, green onions and cilantro. Fold each tortilla in half. In large skillet, heat small amount of oil; quickly fry each folded tortilla on both sides until slightly crisp.

Makes 6 servings

Presentation: Cut each quesadilla into quarters; serve with chunky salsa and guacamole.

Chicken Santiago

2 boneless skinless chicken breasts,
halved (about 1¹/₄ pounds)
Salt and pepper
¹/₃ cup chicken broth or water
¹/₃ cup apple juice
1 tablespoon cornstarch
¹/₄ cup heavy cream
1 cup Chilean red or green seedless
grapes, halved
1 green onion, finely sliced
¹/₄ teaspoon dried thyme leaves
¹/₈ teaspoon ground ginger

Preheat oven to 375°F. Season chicken with salt and pepper. Place in shallow baking dish. Add broth; cover with foil. Bake 20 to 30 minutes or until chicken is tender and juices run clear. Remove chicken; keep warm. Pour ¹/₂ cup pan juices into saucepan. Combine apple juice and cornstarch; add to saucepan and stir well. Add remaining ingredients. Cook over medium-high heat until sauce bubbles and thickens, stirring constantly. *Do not boil.* Season with salt and pepper to taste. Serve sauce over chicken. *Makes 4 servings*

Microwave Directions: Season chicken with salt and pepper. Arrange chicken in round, microwave-safe dish with thickest ends toward outside of dish. Add broth; cover with waxed paper. Microwave at HIGH 6 to 8 minutes or until chicken is tender, turning over and rearranging chicken pieces after 4 minutes. Remove chicken from microwave. Pour ¹/₂ cup pan juices into 2-cup glass measuring cup. Combine apple juice and cornstarch; add to measuring cup and stir well. Add remaining ingredients. Microwave at HIGH 4 to 5 minutes or until sauce bubbles and thickens, stirring twice during cooking. Season and serve as directed.

*Favorite recipe from **Chilean Winter Fruit Association***

Rio Grande Quesadilla

Tortilla Soup

3 corn tortillas (6 to 7 inches in
   diameter)
Vegetable oil
1/2 cup chopped onion
1 small clove garlic, minced
1 can (14 1/2 ounces) tomatoes,
   undrained
2 cans (14 1/2 ounces each) ready-to-
   serve chicken broth *or* 3 1/2 cups
   Basic Chicken Stock (page 118)
1 cup shredded cooked chicken
2 teaspoons lime juice
1 small avocado, halved, peeled,
   pitted and diced
2 tablespoons fresh cilantro leaves

Cut tortillas in half, then crosswise into
1/2-inch strips. Heat 1/2 inch oil in small
skillet over medium-high heat until oil
reaches 360°F; adjust heat to maintain
temperature. Fry tortilla pieces, a few at
a time, 1 minute or until crisp and
lightly browned. Remove with slotted
spoon; drain on paper towels.

Heat 2 teaspoons oil in 3-quart
saucepan over medium heat. Add onion
and garlic; cook until onion is tender.
Coarsely chop tomatoes; add to
saucepan with juice. Add broth. Bring
to a boil; reduce heat. Cover; simmer 15
minutes. Add chicken and lime juice.
Simmer 5 minutes. Serve soup in
individual bowls. Top with avocado,
tortilla strips and cilantro.

Makes 4 servings

Savory Cajun Chicken

1 broiler-fryer chicken, cut up
   (about 3 pounds)
1 tablespoon vegetable oil
1 can (14 1/2 ounces) DEL MONTE®
   Cajun (or Original) Style Stewed
   Tomatoes
1 cup orange juice
1 onion, cut into chunks
3/4 teaspoon dried thyme leaves,
   crushed
1 green bell pepper, cut into strips
1 tablespoon cornstarch
1 tablespoon water

In large skillet over medium-high heat,
brown chicken in oil. Stir in tomatoes,
orange juice, onion and thyme. Cover;
cook 10 minutes. Turn chicken; add
green pepper. Cook 10 minutes or until
chicken is tender and juices run clear.

Dissolve cornstarch in water. Remove
chicken to serving dish; keep warm.
Stir cornstarch mixture into sauce; cook
2 to 3 minutes or until thickened. Pour
sauce over chicken. Serve with hot
cooked rice or pasta, if desired.

Makes 4 to 6 servings

Variation: If using Original Style
Stewed Tomatoes, add a pinch *each* of
ground cinnamon, ground cloves and
ground red pepper.

Prep and Cook Time: 40 minutes

Tortilla Soup

Chicken Cherry-Yaki Stir-Fry

1½ cups tart red cherries, pitted and
　　undrained (frozen or canned)
2 tablespoons teriyaki sauce
2 tablespoons dry sherry
1 tablespoon lemon juice
3 slices fresh ginger (each ¼ inch
　　thick)
2 boneless skinless chicken breasts,
　　cubed (about 1¼ pounds)
2 ounces Chinese rice stick noodles*
　　or 2 cups hot cooked rice
1 tablespoon cornstarch
2 to 3 tablespoons peanut or
　　vegetable oil
6 green onions, diagonally sliced
　　into 1-inch pieces
2 small carrots, thinly sliced
2 cups snow peas
4 ounces sliced water chestnuts,
　　drained
¼ cup slivered toasted almonds for
　　garnish**
4 green onion brushes for garnish

Chicken Cherry-Yaki Stir-Fry

Thaw cherries, if frozen. Drain cherries, reserving juice; set aside. Combine teriyaki sauce, sherry, lemon juice and ginger in small bowl; stir in chicken. Cover; marinate in refrigerator 1 hour, stirring once or twice.

Prepare rice stick noodles according to package directions; drain. Drain chicken, reserving marinade. Discard ginger. Blend reserved cherry juice into cornstarch; stir into marinade and set aside. Heat 2 tablespoons oil in wok or large skillet over high heat. Add sliced green onions, carrots and snow peas; stir-fry 2 to 3 minutes or until crisp-tender. Remove vegetables from wok; add more oil to wok, if needed. Add chicken; stir-fry 2 to 3 minutes or until tender and no longer pink in center. Push chicken away from center of wok; add cornstarch mixture. Cook and stir until thickened and bubbly. Stir in cherries, vegetables and water chestnuts; heat through. Remove chicken mixture from wok. Serve chicken mixture over noodles. Garnish with almonds and green onion brushes.

Serves 4 as a main dish

*If rice stick noodles are fried, keep them warm in oven while preparing stir-fry. If rice stick noodles are soaked, drain them well before serving.

**See page 42 for directions for toasting almonds.

Favorite recipe from New York Cherry Growers Association

Greek-Style Chicken Breasts in Filo

3 boneless skinless chicken breasts, halved (about 2 pounds)
2 tablespoons vegetable oil
¼ cup butter or margarine
1 large onion, chopped
1 can (4 ounces) sliced mushrooms, drained
2 tablespoons parsley flakes
1½ tablespoons finely chopped fresh dill
1 clove garlic, minced
1 package (10 ounces) frozen chopped spinach, cooked and drained
1½ tablespoons all-purpose flour
⅓ cup vermouth
1 cup (8 ounces) POLLY-O® Ricotta Cheese
Salt and pepper
12 sheets filo dough*
½ cup melted butter or margarine
Plain dry bread crumbs

Pound chicken breasts between 2 pieces of plastic wrap to ¼-inch thickness. Heat oil in large skillet over medium heat. Add chicken; cook until browned on both sides. Remove; drain on paper towels and set aside. Wipe out skillet.

Melt ¼ cup butter in same skillet over medium heat. Add onion; cook and stir until golden. Add mushrooms, parsley, dill, garlic and spinach; cook and stir 2 minutes. Stir in flour, mixing well. Gradually stir in vermouth; cook, stirring constantly, until thickened. Stir in ricotta; season with salt and pepper to taste. Remove from heat.

Preheat oven to 350°F. Brush 1 filo sheet with melted butter; sprinkle with crumbs. Cover with 1 filo sheet; brush with melted butter. Place chicken breast half in center of filo; spoon one sixth of spinach mixture on top. Fold filo over chicken, turning ends under. Repeat for each chicken breast half. Place in single layer in greased baking pan. Brush tops with melted butter. Bake 45 minutes or until filo is golden and puffed.

Serves 6 as a main dish

Note: Recipe can be assembled in advance; cover tightly with plastic wrap and refrigerate until ready to bake.

*Keep filo dough tightly covered until ready to use to prevent drying out.

Chicken & Spaghetti Di Napoli

6 slices bacon
6 boneless skinless chicken breast halves (about 2 pounds)
1 cup thinly sliced carrots
1 clove garlic, finely chopped
1 (26-ounce) jar CLASSICO® Di Napoli (Tomato & Basil) Pasta Sauce
1 (1-pound) package CREAMETTE® Spaghetti
2 tablespoons olive or vegetable oil

In large skillet, cook bacon until crisp. Remove; crumble. In same skillet, brown chicken in *2 tablespoons* drippings; remove. Cook and stir carrots and garlic until tender-crisp. Add pasta sauce and chicken. Simmer, uncovered, 10 to 15 minutes or until chicken is tender. Meanwhile, cook spaghetti according to package directions; drain. Toss with oil. Slice chicken; serve on hot cooked spaghetti with sauce. Garnish with bacon. Refrigerate leftovers.

Makes 6 servings

Greek-Style Chicken Breast in Filo

Chicken and Walnut Salad Athena

Hidden Valley Ranch® Lemon
   Herb Dressing (recipe follows)
2 cups cubed cooked chicken breast
2 tablespoons thinly sliced green
   onions
1 tablespoon minced fresh parsley
2 tablespoons butter or margarine
1/2 teaspoon dried rosemary leaves,
   finely crushed
1 cup walnut halves
6 radishes, sliced
12 California ripe olives, sliced
1 cup (4 ounces) fresh feta cheese,
   crumbled
3 small ripe tomatoes, cut into
   wedges
Crisp salad greens

Prepare Hidden Valley Ranch® Lemon
Herb Dressing. Place chicken in large
bowl; pour dressing over chicken. Add
green onions and parsley; mix gently.
Cover; marinate in refrigerator at least
1 hour or overnight.

Melt butter with rosemary in small
heavy skillet over low heat. Add
walnuts; cook, stirring occasionally,

5 minutes or until walnuts are lightly
toasted. Remove from heat; cool.

When ready to serve, add radishes,
olives, cheese and walnuts to chicken
mixture; toss until well mixed. Arrange
chicken mixture and tomatoes on salad
plates lined with salad greens. Garnish
as desired.   *Makes 6 servings*

**Hidden Valley Ranch® Lemon Herb
Dressing:** Place 1/2 cup *each* extra virgin
olive oil and lemon juice, 1 tablespoon
light brown sugar and 1 package (1
ounce) HIDDEN VALLEY RANCH®
Salad Dressing in glass jar with tightly
fitting lid. Cover; shake until well
blended.

Chicken Parisian

1/4 cup unsifted flour
1/4 teaspoon paprika
1/4 teaspoon pepper
6 boneless skinless chicken breast
   halves (about 2 pounds)
3 tablespoons margarine or butter
8 ounces fresh mushrooms, sliced
   (about 2 cups)
1/2 cup water
1/4 cup dry white wine
2 teaspoons WYLER'S® or STEERO®
   Chicken-Flavor Instant Bouillon
   or 2 Chicken-Flavor Bouillon
   Cubes
2 teaspoons chopped fresh parsley
1/4 teaspoon dried thyme leaves

In plastic bag, combine flour, paprika
and pepper. Add chicken, a few pieces
at a time; shake to coat. In skillet,
brown chicken in margarine over
medium-high heat; remove from skillet.
In same skillet, add remaining
ingredients; simmer 3 minutes. Add
chicken; simmer, covered, 20 minutes or
until tender. Refrigerate leftovers.
          Make 6 servings

Chicken and Walnut Salad Athena

Shantung Chicken

2 tablespoons cornstarch, divided
3 tablespoons KIKKOMAN® Soy
  Sauce, divided
1 tablespoon dry sherry
1 clove garlic, minced
1 boneless skinless chicken breast,
  cut into thin strips (about
  10 ounces)
1 cup water
3 tablespoons vegetable oil, divided
½ pound fresh bean sprouts
¼ pound green onions and tops, cut
  into 1½-inch lengths, separating
  whites from tops
1 tablespoon slivered fresh
  ginger root
1 tablespoon sesame seed, toasted*
  Hot cooked noodles

Combine 1 tablespoon each cornstarch
and soy sauce with sherry and garlic in
small bowl; stir in chicken. Let stand
5 minutes. Meanwhile, blend water,
remaining 1 tablespoon cornstarch and
2 tablespoons soy sauce; set aside.

Heat 1 tablespoon oil in hot wok or
large skillet over high heat. Add chicken
and stir-fry 2 minutes; remove. Heat
remaining 2 tablespoons oil in wok.
Add bean sprouts, white parts of green
onions and ginger; stir-fry
3 minutes. Stir in chicken, soy sauce
mixture, green onion tops and sesame
seed. Cook and stir until mixture boils
and thickens. Serve immediately over
noodles.   *Makes 4 servings*

*See page 20 for directions for toasting
sesame seed.

Shantung Chicken

Chicken Pacifica

2 tablespoons vegetable oil
1 broiler-fryer chicken, cut up
  (2½ to 3 pounds)
1 can (8 ounces) pineapple chunks
  in juice, drained (reserve juice)
  Water
1 envelope LIPTON® Onion Recipe
  Soup Mix
2 tablespoons all-purpose flour
¼ cup water

In large skillet over medium-high heat,
heat oil; brown chicken. Combine
reserved juice with enough water to
equal 2 cups; blend in onion recipe
soup mix. Add to skillet and simmer,
covered, stirring occasionally, 45
minutes or until chicken is tender and
juices run clear. Remove chicken to
serving platter; keep warm.

Into skillet, add flour blended with ¼
cup water. Bring to a boil, then simmer,
stirring constantly, until sauce is slightly
thickened, about 5 minutes. Add
pineapple; heat through. Serve sauce
with chicken.   *Makes 4 servings*

Green Enchiladas
with Chicken

1 pound fresh tomatillos* *or* 2 cans
    (13 ounces each) tomatillos,
    drained
1 can (7 ounces) diced green chilies,
    undrained
  Vegetable oil
1 medium onion, finely chopped
1 clove garlic, minced
1 can (14¹/₂ ounces) ready-to-serve
    chicken broth *or* 1³/₄ cups Basic
    Chicken Stock (page 118)
12 corn tortillas (6 to 7 inches in
    diameter)
3 cups shredded cooked chicken
2¹/₂ cups (10 ounces) shredded
    Monterey Jack cheese
1 cup (¹/₂ pint) sour cream
4 green onions with tops, thinly
    sliced
  Cilantro sprigs for garnish

Preheat oven to 350°F. Place tomatillos
and chilies in blender or food processor
container; process until smooth. Heat
2 tablespoons oil in large skillet over
medium heat. Add onion and garlic;
cook until onion is tender. Stir in
tomatillo mixture and broth. Simmer,
uncovered, until sauce is reduced to
about 2¹/₂ cups and is consistency of
canned tomato sauce.

Heat ¹/₂ inch oil in 7- to 8-inch skillet
over medium-high heat. Place 1 tortilla
in hot oil; cook 2 seconds on each side
or just until limp. Drain briefly on
paper towels, then dip softened tortilla
into tomatillo sauce. Transfer dipped
tortilla to plate.

Place about ¹/₄ cup chicken and 2
tablespoons cheese in center of tortilla;
roll to enclose. Place each enchilada,
seam side down, in 15×10-inch baking
pan. Repeat until all tortillas are filled.

Spoon remaining sauce over enchiladas,
moistening all ends; reserve remaining
cheese. Cover.

Bake enchiladas 20 to 30 minutes or
until hot in center. Uncover; top with
reserved cheese. Continue baking,
uncovered, 10 minutes or until cheese is
melted. Garnish enchiladas with sour
cream, green onions and cilantro.

Makes 6 servings

*If using fresh tomatillos, remove
husks; wash thoroughly. Place fresh
tomatillos in 2-quart saucepan; add
¹/₂ inch water. Bring to a boil; reduce
heat. Cover; simmer 10 minutes or until
tender. Drain.

Beijing Chicken

3 pounds frying chicken pieces
¹/₂ cup KIKKOMAN® Teriyaki Sauce
1 tablespoon dry sherry
2 teaspoons minced fresh
    ginger root
¹/₂ teaspoon fennel seed, crushed
¹/₂ teaspoon grated orange peel
¹/₂ teaspoon honey

Rinse chicken pieces and pat dry with
paper towels; place in large plastic bag.
Combine teriyaki sauce, sherry, ginger,
fennel seed, orange peel and honey;
pour over chicken. Press air out of bag;
tie top securely. Refrigerate 8 hours or
overnight, turning bag over occasionally.
Reserving marinade, remove chicken
and place on rack of broiler pan. Broil
5 to 7 inches from heat about 40
minutes, or until chicken is tender,
turning pieces over and basting
occasionally with reserved marinade.

Makes 4 servings

Green Enchiladas with Chicken

Chawan Mushi

peas equally among 4 chawan mushi cups or four 10-ounce custard cups. Pour about ½ cup egg mixture into each cup. Cover with chawan mushi lids, or cover tops tightly with foil or plastic wrap.

Carefully place filled cups on steamer rack. Pour water into large, heavy pan or Dutch oven to a depth of ¾ inch; set rack in pan. Bring water to boil; cover and steam 12 to 15 minutes, or until knife inserted into centers comes out clean.   *Makes 4 side-dish servings*

Chawan Mushi

1 boneless skinless chicken breast
   half (about 5 ounces)
1 tablespoon KIKKOMAN® Soy
   Sauce
½ teaspoon sugar
3 medium mushrooms, sliced
4 eggs
1 bottle (8 ounces) clam juice
¼ cup water
½ teaspoon KIKKOMAN® Soy Sauce
¼ cup fresh or frozen green peas

Cut chicken into 1-inch square pieces. Combine 1 tablespoon soy sauce and sugar in small bowl. Stir in chicken and mushrooms, turning pieces over to coat well. Let stand 15 minutes.

Beat eggs in medium bowl. Gently stir in clam juice, water and ½ teaspoon soy sauce. Divide chicken, mushrooms and

Ravioli and Chicken Parmesano

1 package (12 ounces) fresh or
   frozen cheese ravioli or tortellini
2 cans (14½ ounces each)
   DEL MONTE® Italian Style
   Stewed Tomatoes
½ pound boneless skinless chicken
   breasts or thighs, cut into strips
2 small zucchini, sliced
½ cup chopped onion
2 cloves garlic, crushed
½ teaspoon dried oregano leaves,
   crushed
⅓ cup grated Parmesan cheese

Cook pasta according to package directions; rinse and drain. In large skillet, cook tomatoes, chicken, zucchini, onion, garlic and oregano over medium-high heat 15 minutes or until sauce is thickened and chicken is no longer pink in center, stirring occasionally. Stir in pasta and top with cheese; heat through.

Makes 4 to 6 servings

Prep and Cook Time: 23 minutes

Polynesian Chicken

2½ pounds broiler-fryer chicken pieces
½ cup seasoned all-purpose flour*
¼ cup butter or margarine
1 can (8¼ ounces) pineapple chunks in syrup, undrained
2 tablespoons brown sugar
1 tablespoon vinegar
1¼ cups water
½ teaspoon salt
1½ cups MINUTE® Rice
1 green onion, sliced

Coat chicken with seasoned flour. Brown chicken in hot butter in large skillet. Drain pineapple, reserving ¼ cup syrup. Combine reserved syrup, brown sugar and vinegar in small bowl; pour over chicken. Turn chicken skin-side down; reduce heat. Cover; simmer chicken until fork tender, about 20 minutes. Move chicken to side of skillet.

Add pineapple, water and salt. Bring to a full boil. Stir in rice. Cover; remove from heat. Let stand 5 minutes. Fluff with fork. Garnish with green onion.

Makes 4 servings

*Flour may be seasoned with ¼ teaspoon each pepper and ground nutmeg or ½ teaspoon paprika and ¼ teaspoon ground ginger.

Polynesian Chicken

Curried Chicken Calcutta

**2 boneless skinless chicken breasts,
 halved (about 1¼ pounds)**
¼ cup all-purpose flour
½ teaspoon curry powder
½ teaspoon ground cinnamon
½ teaspoon ground ginger
¼ teaspoon garlic powder
¼ cup vegetable oil
1 cup plain yogurt
2 tablespoons lime juice
Grated peel of 1 lime
Lime slices for garnish
Mint sprigs for garnish

Combine flour and seasonings in shallow dish. Add chicken, one piece at a time, dredging to coat. Heat oil in large skillet over medium heat. Add chicken; cook until browned on both sides. Reduce heat to low. Cover; cook 15 minutes or until chicken is tender and juices run clear.

Combine yogurt and lime juice in small saucepan. Cook over low heat, stirring constantly, until warm. Arrange chicken on serving platter. Spoon half of yogurt sauce over chicken; sprinkle with grated lime peel. Garnish with lime slices and mint. Pass remaining yogurt sauce.

Makes 4 servings

*Favorite recipe from **Delmarva Poultry Industry, Inc.***

Curried Chicken Calcutta

Chilaquiles

1 can (10¾ ounces) condensed cream
    of chicken soup
½ cup prepared mild green salsa
1 can (4 ounces) diced green chilies,
    undrained
8 cups taco chips (about 24 ounces)
2 to 3 cups shredded cooked chicken
2 cups (8 ounces) shredded Cheddar
    cheese
   Sliced pitted ripe olives and
    cilantro sprigs for garnish

Preheat oven to 300°F. Combine soup,
salsa and chilies in medium bowl. Place
one third of tortilla chips in 2- to 2½-
quart casserole dish; top with one third
of chicken. Spread one third of soup
mixture over chicken; sprinkle with one
third of cheese. Repeat layers. Bake,
uncovered, 15 minutes or until heated
through and cheese melts. Garnish with
olives and cilantro.

Makes 6 servings

Chicken Cashew

1 pound skinned boneless chicken
    breasts, cut into chunks
2 teaspoons WYLER'S® or STEERO®
    Chicken-Flavor Instant Bouillon
    or 2 Chicken-Flavor Bouillon
    Cubes
1¼ cups boiling water
2 tablespoons soy sauce
1 tablespoon cornstarch
2 teaspoons light brown sugar
½ teaspoon ground ginger
2 tablespoons vegetable oil
8 ounces fresh mushrooms, sliced
½ cup sliced green onions
1 green bell pepper, sliced
1 (8-ounce) can sliced water
    chestnuts, drained
½ cup cashews
   Hot cooked rice

Chicken Cashew

In small saucepan, dissolve bouillon in
water. Combine soy sauce, cornstarch,
sugar and ginger; stir into bouillon
mixture. In large skillet, brown chicken
in oil. Add bouillon mixture; cook and
stir until slightly thickened. Add
remaining ingredients except cashews
and rice; simmer, uncovered, 5 to 8
minutes, or until chicken is done,
stirring occasionally. Remove from heat;
add ¼ *cup* cashews. Serve over rice.
Garnish with remaining ¼ *cup* cashews.
Refrigerate leftovers.   *Makes 4 servings*

Chicken Couscous

1½ cups couscous*
3½ cups chicken broth, divided
6 tablespoons butter or margarine, divided
1 cup chopped onion
2 tomatoes, peeled and cubed
2 carrots, pared and diagonally sliced
1 green bell pepper, cut into strips
½ small butternut squash, pared and cubed (2 cups)
1 teaspoon salt
2 cups cubed cooked chicken
1 zucchini, sliced
1 can (20 ounces) chickpeas, drained
½ cup raisins
1 teaspoon lemon juice
½ teaspoon ground cinnamon
½ teaspoon TABASCO® Pepper Sauce
¼ teaspoon ground turmeric
¼ teaspoon paprika
Hot Sauce (recipe follows)

Place couscous in medium bowl. Add 1½ cups broth; soak 20 minutes or until all broth is absorbed. Rub couscous between fingers to remove any lumps. Place in colander over simmering water. Cover; let steam 1 hour. In large saucepan, melt 3 tablespoons butter over medium-high heat; sauté onion until tender. Add tomatoes, carrots, green pepper, squash and salt. Reduce heat to low. Cover; cook 30 minutes. Add 1 cup chicken broth, chicken, zucchini, chickpeas, raisins, lemon juice, cinnamon, Tabasco® sauce, turmeric and paprika. Cook 10 minutes. Reserve 1 cup broth drained from chicken-vegetable mixture to make Hot Sauce. Add remaining 3 tablespoons butter to couscous; mix well. Serve couscous with chicken-vegetable mixture, Hot Sauce and remaining 1 cup broth, heated.   *Makes 6 servings*

Hot Sauce

1 cup reserved chicken broth drained from chicken-vegetable mixture
½ to ¾ teaspoon TABASCO® Pepper Sauce
½ teaspoon paprika

Combine all ingredients in small bowl.

*If using quick-cooking couscous, cook according to package directions and omit steaming step.

Chicken & Pasta Sicilian

4 to 6 boneless chicken breast halves, lightly seasoned and coated with flour and paprika (1¼ to 2 pounds)
Vegetable or olive oil
½ (1-pound) package CREAMETTE® Spaghetti or Fettuccini, cooked and drained
⅓ cup chopped walnuts, toasted
¼ cup margarine or butter, melted
1 (26-ounce) jar CLASSICO® Di Sicilia (Ripe Olives & Mushrooms) Pasta Sauce, heated

In large skillet, cook chicken breasts in oil until tender and golden on both sides. Slice crosswise; set aside. Toss together hot cooked pasta, walnuts and margarine. Spoon hot pasta sauce over chicken. Serve with pasta. Garnish with fresh basil, if desired. Refrigerate leftovers.   *Makes 4 to 6 servings*

Chicken & Pasta Sicilian

Chicken Tabbouleh

1 cup bulgur or cracked wheat
3 cups hot water
1½ to 2 pounds boneless skinless
    chicken breasts or thighs, cut
    into ½-inch cubes
1 teaspoon salt, divided
¼ teaspoon pepper, divided
2 teaspoons olive or vegetable oil
1 teaspoon butter or margarine
1 to 2 cups minced fresh parsley
¼ cup finely chopped onion
½ cup olive or vegetable oil
7 tablespoons fresh lemon juice
¼ teaspoon garlic powder
    Thin lemon slices for garnish

Soak bulgur in hot water in medium
bowl 30 minutes.

Sprinkle chicken with ½ teaspoon salt
and ⅛ teaspoon pepper. Heat 2
teaspoons oil and butter in large skillet
over medium heat. Add chicken; cook,
stirring frequently, until chicken is no
longer pink in center, 3 to 5 minutes.
Set aside.

Chicken Tabbouleh

Drain bulgur; transfer to large bowl.
Add chicken, parsley, onion, ½ cup oil,
lemon juice, remaining ½ teaspoon salt,
remaining ⅛ teaspoon pepper and
garlic powder. Toss well. Cover;
refrigerate at least 1 hour. Garnish with
lemon slices.

Makes 4 main-dish servings

Citrus Chicken Iberia

1 broiler-fryer chicken, quartered
    (2½ to 3½ pounds)
2 tablespoons all-purpose flour
½ teaspoon salt
⅛ teaspoon black pepper
2 tablespoons butter or margarine
2 tablespoons olive oil
1 clove garlic, minced
1 can (6 ounces) Florida frozen
    orange juice concentrate,
    thawed, undiluted
½ cup chicken broth or water
1 teaspoon dried oregano leaves
1 green bell pepper, cut into strips
1 red onion, sliced
½ pound mushrooms, cut into slices
½ cup sliced pitted ripe olives

Wash chicken; pat dry. Combine flour,
salt and black pepper. Dredge chicken
in flour mixture. In large skillet, heat
butter and oil over medium-high heat;
sauté garlic until lightly browned. Add
chicken; cook until browned on both
sides.

Combine orange juice concentrate, broth
and oregano; pour over chicken. Cover;
cook 15 minutes. Baste chicken with
pan juices. Add green pepper and
onion. Cover; cook 5 minutes. Add
mushrooms and olives. Cover; cook 5
minutes or until chicken is tender and
juices run clear.   *Makes 4 servings*

*Favorite recipe from **Florida Department of Citrus***

Caribbean Pineapple Chicken

Caribbean Pineapple Chicken

1 DOLE® Fresh Pineapple
1 tablespoon vegetable oil
1 boneless skinless chicken breast,
    halved (about 10 ounces)
1 clove garlic, pressed
2 teaspoons all-purpose flour
1/4 cup water
2 to 3 tablespoons honey
1 to 2 tablespoons soy sauce
    Grated peel and juice of 1 lime
1/4 teaspoon coconut extract
    Pinch ground red pepper
1 tablespoon flaked coconut
    (optional)
1 to 2 teaspoons minced fresh
    cilantro *or* green onions
    (optional)

- Twist crown from pineapple. Cut pineapple in half lengthwise. Refrigerate half for another use. Cut fruit from shell with knife. Cut fruit crosswise into 6 slices.

- In 8-inch nonstick skillet, sauté pineapple in oil over medium-high heat until slightly browned. Remove to plates.

- Rub chicken with garlic; sprinkle with flour. In same skillet, sauté chicken, covered, in pan juices over medium-high heat until browned; turn once.

- Mix water, honey, soy sauce, lime juice, coconut extract and ground red pepper in cup; pour into skillet. Cover; simmer 12 to 15 minutes or until chicken is tender. Remove chicken to serving plates.

- Arrange chicken on plates. Spoon sauce over top. Sprinkle with coconut, lime peel and cilantro.

Makes 2 servings

Prep and Cook Time: 30 minutes

Indian Chicken Crêpes

1½ cups chopped cooked chicken
1 carton (8 ounces) plain low fat
    yogurt
2 tablespoons raisins
2 tablespoons sliced green onion
2 tablespoons chopped sweet pickle
½ to 1 teaspoon curry powder
    (optional)
⅛ teaspoon ground red pepper
¾ cup QUAKER® Oat Bran hot
    cereal, uncooked
1 teaspoon baking powder
1 cup skim milk
3 egg whites, slightly beaten
1 tablespoon liquid vegetable oil
    margarine
⅓ cup chopped dry roasted peanuts

Combine chicken, yogurt, raisins, onion, pickle, curry powder and ground red pepper; mix well. Cover; chill.

Combine oat bran and baking powder; add combined milk, egg whites and margarine, mixing well. Heat 6- to 7-inch crêpe pan or skillet over medium heat. Lightly spray with vegetable oil cooking spray, or oil lightly, before making each crêpe. Pour about ¼ cup batter onto hot prepared pan; immediately tilt pan to coat bottom evenly. Cook 1 to 1½ minutes or until *top looks dry*. Turn crêpe over; cook an additional 1 minute. Cool. Repeat with remaining batter. Stack between sheets of waxed paper.

Stir peanuts into chicken mixture just before serving. Spoon about 2 tablespoons filling along less evenly browned side of each crêpe. Fold or roll up sides to cover filling. Serve immediately. Garnish as desired.

Makes 5 servings

Spicy Thai-Style Chicken and Rice

5 boneless skinless chicken breast
    halves (about 1½ pounds)
¼ cup reduced-sodium soy sauce
2 teaspoons peanut or vegetable oil
1 cup UNCLE BEN'S®
    CONVERTED® Brand Rice
1 large clove garlic, minced
2¼ cups chicken broth
2 tablespoons creamy peanut butter
½ teaspoon crushed red pepper
    flakes *or* ¼ teaspoon ground
    red pepper
1½ cups pea pods (cut in half, if
    large)
1 tablespoon finely grated fresh
    ginger
1 small red bell pepper, cut into
    short, thin strips
2 tablespoons peanut halves
    (optional)

Combine chicken and soy sauce in shallow bowl; set aside. Heat oil in 10-inch skillet over medium heat. Add rice and garlic; cook and stir 1 minute. Stir in broth, peanut butter and pepper flakes. Bring to a boil, stirring until peanut butter is melted. Place chicken over rice mixture, adding soy sauce to skillet; reduce heat. Cover; simmer 20 minutes or until chicken is tender. Stir in pea pods and ginger; sprinkle with pepper strips. Remove from heat. Let stand, covered, until all liquid is absorbed, about 5 minutes. Sprinkle with peanuts, if desired.

Makes 5 servings

Indian Chicken Crêpes

Russian Chicken with Gooseberry Sauce

Russian Chicken with Gooseberry Sauce

1 broiler-fryer chicken, quartered (about 3 pounds)
1 teaspoon salt
¼ teaspoon dried thyme leaves
¼ teaspoon dried rosemary leaves
¼ teaspoon dried oregano leaves
1 can (16 ounces) gooseberries in light syrup*
2 tablespoons all-purpose flour
2 tablespoons butter
2 tablespoons white wine
1¾ cups chicken broth, heated

Mix together salt, thyme, rosemary and oregano; rub mixture on chicken. Arrange chicken on rack in baking pan. Bake in 375°F oven 45 minutes or until fork can be inserted into chicken with ease. Remove chicken to warm platter. Pour off fat; reserve remainder of pan drippings.

Drain gooseberries well, reserving ¼ cup syrup. Brown flour in ungreased skillet over medium heat, stirring, about 2 minutes. Add butter; stir until melted. Add gooseberry syrup and wine to hot broth in separate, small saucepan; slowly pour into skillet, stirring until thickened and bubbly. Add reserved pan drippings and gooseberries, then add chicken, spooning gooseberries gently over all. Simmer about 3 minutes. Arrange chicken on serving platter; spoon sauce over chicken. Garnish as desired.   *Makes 4 servings*

*Gooseberries are firm, round berries that have a distinctly tart flavor. Canned gooseberries benefit from the sweetness of the syrup; therefore, it is not recommended that this recipe be prepared using fresh gooseberries. Canned gooseberries can be found in gourmet food shops or shops specializing in jams and jellies.

Favorite recipe from **National Broiler Council**

Olympic Seoul Chicken

8 skinless chicken thighs (about
   2 pounds)
$1/4$ cup white vinegar
3 tablespoons soy sauce
2 tablespoons honey
$1/4$ teaspoon ground ginger
2 tablespoons peanut oil
10 cloves garlic, coarsely chopped
$1/2$ to 1 teaspoon crushed red pepper
2 ounces Chinese rice stick noodles*
   or 2 cups hot cooked rice

Combine vinegar, soy sauce, honey and ginger in small bowl; set aside. Heat oil in large skillet over medium-high heat. Add chicken; cook about 10 minutes or until evenly browned on both sides.

Add garlic and red pepper; cook, stirring often, 2 to 3 minutes. Drain off excess fat. Add vinegar mixture; reduce heat. Cover; simmer about 15 minutes or until chicken is tender and juices run clear. Meanwhile, prepare rice stick noodles according to package directions.

Uncover chicken; cook about 2 minutes or until sauce is reduced and thickened. Serve with noodles and desired vegetables.   *Serves 4 as a main dish*

*If rice stick noodles are fried, keep warm in oven while preparing stir-fry. If rice stick noodles are soaked, drain well before serving.

*Favorite recipe from **Delmarva Poultry Industry, Inc.***

Olympic Seoul Chicken

Fresh Gazpacho Chicken

2 chicken breasts, halved (about
    1½ pounds)
¼ cup all-purpose flour
1½ teaspoons salt, divided
½ teaspoon paprika
¼ teaspoon black pepper, divided
¼ cup vegetable oil
2½ cups tomato juice
½ cup finely chopped seeded
    tomatoes
½ cup finely chopped carrots
½ cup finely chopped celery
½ cup finely chopped onion
½ cup finely chopped green bell
    pepper
½ cup finely chopped, peeled and
    seeded cucumber
½ cup red wine vinegar
¼ cup olive oil
5 teaspoons Worcestershire sauce
5 dashes hot pepper sauce
2 cloves garlic, crushed
  Hot cooked rice

Combine flour, 1 teaspoon salt, paprika
and ⅛ teaspoon black pepper in
shallow dish. Add chicken, one piece at
a time, dredging to coat. Heat vegetable
oil in large skillet over medium heat;
add chicken. Cook about 10 minutes or
until browned on both sides; drain
off oil.

Combine remaining ingredients, except
rice, in large bowl. Stir in remaining ½
teaspoon salt and ⅛ teaspoon black
pepper. Reserve 1 cup tomato mixture;
cover and refrigerate. Pour remaining
tomato mixture over chicken in skillet.
Cover; cook over medium heat, turning
occasionally, about 30 minutes or until
chicken is tender and juices run clear.
Arrange chicken on serving platter;
spoon about 1 cup pan juices over
chicken. Serve with chilled tomato
mixture and rice. Garnish as desired.

Makes 4 servings

*Favorite recipe from **Delmarva Poultry Industry, Inc.***

Chicken Français

1 broiler-fryer chicken, cut up (2 to
    3 pounds)
1 tablespoon vegetable oil
1 large onion, chopped
2 cloves garlic, minced
1 can (16 ounces) tomatoes,
    undrained
1 cup chicken broth
¼ pound cooked ham, cut into strips
½ teaspoon TABASCO® Pepper Sauce
½ teaspoon ground cinnamon
  Pinch ground cloves
  Pinch ground nutmeg
4 large carrots, cut into 1-inch pieces
1 bunch green onions, cut into
    2-inch pieces
  Hot cooked rice (optional)

In large skillet over medium-high heat,
brown chicken in hot oil about 10
minutes; remove. In same skillet, cook
onion and garlic 5 minutes or until
golden. Stir in tomatoes with juice,
broth, ham, Tabasco® sauce, cinnamon,
cloves and nutmeg. Return chicken to
skillet. Add carrots and green onions.

Reduce heat to medium. Cover; simmer
35 minutes or until chicken and
vegetables are tender. Remove chicken,
ham and vegetables to serving platter;
keep warm. Cook pan juices,
uncovered, over high heat until reduced
by half. Spoon over chicken. Serve with
rice. *Makes 4 servings*

Fresh Gazpacho Chicken

Chicken Columbia

2 medium, green-tip DOLE®
    Bananas, peeled
2 tablespoons vegetable oil, divided
2 boneless skinless chicken breasts,
    halved (about 1¼ pounds)
2 cloves garlic, minced
2 tablespoons minced ginger root
    Orange peel strips*
½ cup orange juice
½ cup water, divided
2 tablespoons chopped chutney
2 teaspoons cornstarch

- Cut bananas in half crosswise, then lengthwise. In medium skillet, sauté bananas in 1 tablespoon oil over medium-high heat 30 to 45 seconds, shaking skillet. Remove from skillet.

- Add remaining 1 tablespoon oil to skillet. Brown chicken on both sides in hot oil. Add garlic and ginger root; sauté. Stir in orange peel and juice, ¼ cup water and chutney. Cover; simmer 20 minutes.

- Mix cornstarch and remaining ¼ cup water; stir into pan juices. Cook until sauce boils and thickens.

- Serve chicken with bananas. Generously spoon sauce over chicken.

Makes 4 servings

*Use vegetable peeler to cut thin strips from orange.

Chicken Columbia

Mongolian Pot

4 tablespoons KIKKOMAN® Soy
    Sauce, divided
2 teaspoons minced fresh
    ginger root
½ teaspoon sugar
2 boneless skinless chicken breasts,
    cut into thin strips (about
    1¼ pounds)
2 cans (10¼ ounces each) condensed
    chicken broth
4 soup cans water
1 large clove garlic, minced
½ pound cabbage, cut into ¾-inch
    chunks (about 4 cups)
¾ pound fresh spinach, trimmed,
    washed and drained
3 green onions and tops, cut into
    1-inch lengths and slivered
4 ounces vermicelli or thin
    spaghetti, cooked and drained
¼ pound mushrooms, sliced

Combine 2 tablespoons soy sauce, ginger and sugar in medium dish; stir in chicken. Let stand 15 minutes.

Meanwhile, combine broth, water, remaining 2 tablespoons soy sauce and garlic in deep electric skillet or electric wok; bring to boil. Reduce heat; keep broth mixture hot. Arrange cabbage, spinach, green onions, vermicelli and mushrooms on platter. Using chopsticks or tongs, let individuals select and add chicken, vegetables and vermicelli to hot broth. Cook chicken until tender, vegetables to desired doneness and vermicelli until heated through. Serve in individual bowls with additional soy sauce, as desired. When all foods are cooked, serve broth as soup.

Makes 4 to 6 servings

Chicken Taquitos

Chicken Taquitos

12 corn tortillas
 **1 pound boneless skinless chicken
    breasts, cooked and shredded**
 **1 package (1.25 ounces) LAWRY'S®
    Taco Spices & Seasonings**
¹⁄₂ cup hot water
¹⁄₂ cup minced green onions
**¹⁄₄ teaspoon LAWRY'S® Garlic Powder
    with Parsley**
 **1 cup finely chopped tomatoes
    Vegetable oil**

Sprinkle tortillas lightly with water;
wrap in aluminum foil and place in
200°F oven 10 minutes to soften. Leave
in foil until ready to use.

In skillet, combine chicken, Taco Spices
& Seasonings, water, green onions and
Garlic Powder with Parsley; blend well.
Bring to a boil; reduce heat and simmer
10 minutes. Stir in tomatoes. Place 2

tablespoons chicken mixture in center of
each warmed tortilla. Roll up tortillas
tightly; secure with wooden toothpicks.

In large, deep saucepan, heat oil to
375°F. Fry rolled tortillas in oil until
golden brown and crisp. Drain well on
paper towels. Keep warm in oven;
remove toothpicks before serving.

Makes 6 servings

Presentation: Serve on shredded
lettuce. Garnish with guacamole and
sliced red onion.

Microwave Directions: Sprinkle tortillas
lightly with water. Wrap in plastic;
microwave on HIGH 30 seconds to
soften. Leave in plastic until ready to
use. In large, microwave-safe dish,
combine chicken, Taco Spices &
Seasonings, water, green onions and
Garlic Powder with Parsley; blend well.
Cover; microwave on HIGH 5 to 6
minutes, stirring after 4 minutes. Stir in
tomatoes. Fill, roll and fry tortillas as
directed.

FROM THE GRILL

Fire up casual get-togethers with these outdoor-cooking creations. Ranch Chicken or Kansas City-Style Barbecued Chicken Legs are sure to win raves.

Zingy Barbecued Chicken

 1 broiler-fryer chicken, cut up
  (2½ to 3½ pounds)
½ cup grapefruit juice
½ cup apple cider vinegar
½ cup vegetable oil
¼ cup chopped onion
 1 egg
½ teaspoon celery salt
½ teaspoon ground ginger
⅛ teaspoon pepper

In blender container, process all ingredients, except chicken, 30 seconds. Pour sauce into small saucepan; heat 5 minutes until slightly thickened. Dip chicken in sauce, coating thoroughly. Reserve sauce.

Place chicken on prepared grill, skin side down, 8 inches from heat. Grill, turning every 10 minutes, for 50 minutes until chicken is tender. Brush with reserved sauce during last 20 minutes of grilling. (Watch chicken carefully; egg in sauce may cause chicken to overbrown.)

Makes 4 servings

Favorite recipe from **National Broiler Council**

Chicken Kyoto

 1 cup apple cider
½ cup soy sauce
½ cup vegetable oil
¼ cup sugar
 2 teaspoons ground ginger
 1 broiler-fryer chicken, quartered
  (2 to 3 pounds)

In small saucepan, combine all ingredients except chicken. Simmer over medium heat 5 to 8 minutes or until sugar is dissolved; cool slightly. Place chicken in shallow glass dish. Pour marinade over chicken; cover and refrigerate about 6 hours. Drain chicken; reserve marinade. Grill chicken, on uncovered grill, over medium-hot KINGSFORD® briquets, 15 to 20 minutes on each side, basting often with marinade, until fork-tender.

Makes 4 to 6 servings

Zingy Barbecued Chicken

GRILLING BASICS

• Watch grilled chicken closely for doneness. The position of chicken pieces on the grill, temperature of the coals and weather can affect cooking time. Also consider *what* you're grilling—kabobs, burgers and boneless chicken cook more quickly than quartered, halved and whole bone-in chicken.

• To grill using **direct heat**, arrange hot coals directly under chicken in single layer. Burgers, kabobs and boneless chicken cook best using this method. To grill using **indirect heat**, arrange hot coals to one side of grill; place drip pan under chicken on opposite side of grill. Whole, halved and quartered chicken cook best using this method. (For hotter coals using indirect heat method, divide and place hot coals evenly on opposite sides of grill with drip pan in center.)

• The easiest way to check coal temperature is to hold your hand cautiously at grid level—over the coals for direct heat and over the drip pan for indirect heat—and count the number of seconds that you can do so comfortably.

   2 seconds = **hot** (at least 375°F)
   3 seconds = **medium-hot** (350°F to 375°F)
   4 seconds = **medium** (300°F to 350°F)
   5 seconds = **low** (200°F or less)

• Use caution when burning mesquite charcoal; it burns hotter and cooks faster than other types of charcoal. Let mesquite charcoal burn until coals are covered with gray ash before placing chicken on grill; do not tap off ash.

MARINADES AND SAUCES
• Always marinate chicken in refrigerator if marinating time exceeds 20 minutes. Large, resealable plastic bags make excellent marinating containers.

• Marinades used as basting sauces should only be applied *up to* the last 5 minutes of grilling. This precaution is necessary because the marinade could have become contaminated with harmful bacteria from the chicken during the marinating process. The marinade must be cooked over heat for a minimum of 5 minutes to ensure that harmful bacteria are destroyed. The safest way to apply basting sauce is to brush it on the chicken before turning it over. This way, the marinade is on the side exposed directly to heat.

• Marinades used as dipping sauces should be boiled for at least 1 full minute on the range *before* serving to eliminate any harmful bacteria.

• If your basting sauce contains sugar, honey, egg yolk or tomato products, delay basting chicken until the last 15 minutes of grilling to prevent sauce from charring or overbrowning.

QUICK TIPS
• Coating grill rack with vegetable oil or vegetable oil cooking spray often simplifies cleanup later.

• When turning or moving chicken on grill, use long-handled tongs or spatula; forks and knives can puncture meat and allow flavorful juices to escape.

• If using wooden or bamboo skewers for kabobs, soak them in water for at least 20 minutes before using to prevent them from scorching or igniting on the grill.

• To prevent charring, always remove any visible fat from chicken before grilling.

• Always transfer grilled chicken to a clean plate, *never* to the plate that held the raw chicken.

Honey 'n' Spice Chicken Kabobs

1 medium green bell pepper, cut
  into 1-inch squares
2 boneless skinless chicken breasts,
  halved (about 1¼ pounds)
1 can (8 ounces) pineapple chunks,
  drained
½ cup HEINZ® 57 Sauce
¼ cup honey
  Melted butter or margarine

In small saucepan, blanch green pepper in boiling water 1 minute; drain. Cut each chicken breast half into 4 pieces. Alternately thread chicken, green pepper and pineapple onto skewers. In small bowl, combine 57 Sauce and honey. Brush kabobs with butter, then 57 Sauce mixture. Grill or broil kabobs, about 6 inches from heat, 12 to 14 minutes or until chicken is tender and no longer pink in center, turning and brushing with 57 Sauce mixture once.

Makes 4 servings

Honey 'n' Spice Chicken Kabobs

Grilled Chicken Salad

3/4 **pound boneless skinless chicken breast**
1/2 **teaspoon salt**
1/2 **teaspoon ground black pepper**
1 1/2 **cups diagonally sliced small zucchini**
3 **cups cooked rice, cooled to room temperature**
1 **can (14 ounces) artichoke hearts, drained**
3/4 **cup fresh snow peas, blanched***
1/2 **medium red bell pepper, cut into 1-inch cubes**
Lettuce leaves
1/3 **cup light Italian salad dressing**
1 **teaspoon chopped fresh basil leaves**

Season chicken with salt and black pepper. Grill or broil chicken breast. Add zucchini during last 5 minutes of grilling or broiling. Cover and chill chicken and zucchini; cut chicken into 3/4-inch slices. Arrange rice, chicken, zucchini, artichokes, snow peas, and red pepper over lettuce leaves on serving platter or individual salad plates. Blend dressing and basil in small bowl; pour over salad.

Makes 4 servings

*To blanch snow peas, cook peas in boiling water to cover for 1 to 2 minutes; plunge immediately into cold water. Drain peas well before continuing. Or, substitute frozen snow peas, thawed, for fresh snow peas, if desired.

Favorite recipe from **USA Rice Council**

Mexican Chicken with Spicy Bacon

2 **serrano chili peppers,*stemmed**
2 **cloves garlic, finely chopped**
Dash ground cinnamon
Dash ground cloves
1 **whole roasting chicken (3 1/2 to 4 pounds)**
4 **slices bacon, partially cooked, cut into 1-inch pieces**

Remove and discard seeds and ribs from chilies. Mince chilies; combine in small bowl with garlic, cinnamon and cloves.

At neck cavity, lift skin of chicken from meat along breast, thigh and drumstick. Work finger between skin and meat to form pockets. Using small metal spatula, spread pepper mixture evenly into pockets; massage outer skin to spread pepper mixture. Place bacon pieces over pepper mixture in pockets. Skewer neck skin to back. Tie legs securely to tail and twist wing tips under back of chicken. Insert meat thermometer in center of thigh muscle, not touching bone.

Arrange medium-hot KINGSFORD® briquets around drip pan. Place chicken, breast side up, over drip pan; grill, covered, about 1 hour or until meat thermometer registers 185°F. Garnish as desired. *Makes 4 servings*

*Chilies contain volatile oils which may burn your skin or make your eyes smart. When handling chilies, it is best to wear rubber gloves and avoid touching your face or eyes. Thoroughly wash any skin that comes into direct contact with chilies.

Grilled Chicken Salad

Chicken Scandia

1 jar (12 ounces) HEINZ® HomeStyle
    Chicken Gravy
1/4 cup dairy sour cream
2 teaspoons lemon juice
1 teaspoon dried dill weed
2 boneless skinless chicken breasts,
    halved, grilled (about
    1¼ pounds)
Hot cooked noodles

In small saucepan, combine gravy, sour
cream, lemon juice and dill; heat over
low heat, stirring, until smooth and
warm. *Do not boil.* For each serving,
slice chicken diagonally across grain
into 4 slices. Arrange on bed of noodles;
spoon gravy mixture over chicken.
Garnish with lemon wedges, if desired.
Makes 4 servings

Grilled Lemon Chicken

1/4 cup fresh lemon juice
1 tablespoon minced onion
1 teaspoon grated lemon peel
1 teaspoon salt
1/2 teaspoon dried tarragon leaves,
    crushed
1/2 teaspoon paprika
4 to 5 drops hot pepper sauce
1 broiler-fryer chicken, quartered
    (2 to 3 pounds)

Combine all ingredients except chicken.
Arrange chicken in shallow glass dish.
Pour marinade over chicken; cover and
refrigerate 2 to 4 hours. Drain chicken;
reserve marinade. Grill chicken, on
covered, greased grill, over medium-hot
KINGSFORD® briquets, 15 to 20
minutes on each side, basting often
with reserved marinade, until fork-
tender. *Makes 4 servings*

Tandoori-Style Chicken Kabobs

1/2 pint (8 ounces) plain yogurt
1/2 cup WISH-BONE® Italian
    Dressing
1 tablespoon chopped fresh ginger
    or 1/2 teaspoon ground ginger
1 teaspoon cumin seed *or*
    1/2 teaspoon ground cumin
1 teaspoon coriander seed (optional)
1/2 teaspoon paprika
1 pound boneless chicken breasts,
    cut into 1-inch pieces
Tandoori Rice (recipe follows)

In blender or food processor container,
process yogurt, Italian Dressing, ginger,
cumin seed, coriander seed and paprika
until well blended. In large, shallow
baking dish, combine chicken with
dressing mixture. Cover; marinate in
refrigerator, stirring occasionally, at least
3 hours. Remove chicken, reserving
marinade.

Thread chicken onto skewers. Grill or
broil, turning and basting occasionally
with reserved marinade, 5 minutes or
until chicken is tender and no longer
pink in center. Serve with Tandoori
Rice. *Makes 8 servings*

Tandoori Rice: In medium saucepan,
bring 2 cups water, 1/4 cup chopped
onion, 2 tablespoons butter or
margarine, 2 tablespoons brown sugar,
1/2 teaspoon salt, 1/2 teaspoon ground
cinnamon, 1/2 teaspoon coriander seed
(optional), 1/2 teaspoon ground
cardamom and 1/4 teaspoon ground
cloves to a boil. Stir in 1 cup uncooked
regular rice and simmer, covered, 20
minutes or until rice is tender.

•Also terrific with Wish-Bone® Robusto
Italian, Blended Italian, Lite Italian, or
Lite Classic Dijon Vinaigrette Dressing.

Sweet and Spicy Chicken Barbecue

1½ cups DOLE® Pineapple Orange
    Juice
  1 cup orange marmalade
  ⅔ cup teriyaki sauce
  ½ cup firmly packed brown sugar
  ½ teaspoon ground cloves
  ½ teaspoon ground ginger
  4 broiler-fryer chickens, halved or
    quartered (about 2 pounds each)
    Salt and pepper
  1 can (20 ounces) DOLE® Pineapple
    slices, drained
  4 teaspoons cornstarch

- In saucepan, combine juice,
  marmalade, teriyaki sauce, brown
  sugar, cloves and ginger. Heat over
  medium heat until sugar dissolves; let
  cool. Sprinkle chicken with salt and
  pepper. Place chicken in glass baking
  pan. Pour juice mixture over chicken;
  turn to coat all sides. Marinate,
  covered, 2 hours in refrigerator,
  turning often.

- Preheat oven to 350°F. Light charcoal
  grill. Drain chicken; reserve marinade.
  Bake chicken 20 minutes. Arrange
  chicken on lightly greased grill, 4 to
  6 inches above glowing coals. Grill,
  turning and basting often with
  reserved marinade, 20 to 25 minutes
  or until meat near bone is no longer
  pink. Grill pineapple slices 3 minutes
  or until heated through.

- In small saucepan, dissolve cornstarch
  in remaining marinade. Cook over
  medium heat until sauce boils and
  thickens. Spoon over chicken. Serve
  chicken with pineapple.

Makes 8 servings

Sweet and Spicy Chicken Barbecue

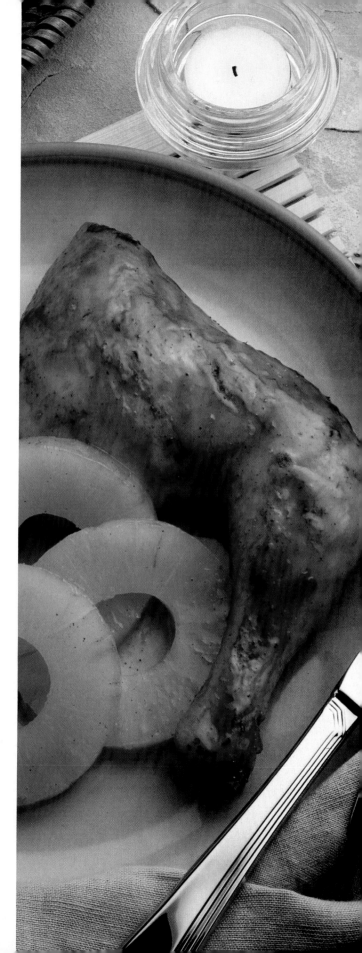

Grilled Chicken Skewers

½ **pound boneless skinless chicken**
   breasts, cut into thin strips
½ **pound bacon slices**
⅓ **cup lemon juice**
⅓ **cup honey**
1½ **teaspoons LAWRY'S® Lemon**
   Pepper Seasoning
½ **teaspoon LAWRY'S® Seasoned Salt**

Thread chicken strips and bacon slices onto wooden skewers. In shallow, oblong dish, combine remaining ingredients. Add prepared skewers; brush with marinade to coat. Refrigerate 1 hour or overnight. Remove chicken; reserve marinade. Grill or broil chicken 10 to 15 minutes, basting with reserved marinade, until chicken is no longer pink in center and bacon is crisp.

Makes 2 servings

Presentation: Garnish with lemon wedges. Serve as a light entrée or divide and serve as appetizers.

Hint: Soak wooden skewers in water before adding chicken and bacon to prevent skewers from burning.

Grilled Chicken Skewers

Barbecued Chicken on a Bun

1 teaspoon seasoned salt
1/8 teaspoon coarsely ground black pepper
2 boneless chicken breasts, halved (about 1 1/4 pounds)
4 buns, split and toasted
4 slices Swiss cheese (4 ounces)
4 slices baked ham, warmed (4 ounces)
  Peach-Mint Salsa (recipe follows)
  Lettuce leaves
  Savory Grilled Peaches (recipe follows)

Combine seasoned salt and pepper. Loosen one edge of skin of each chicken breast half; rub one fourth of seasoning mixture underneath skin. Cook chicken, skin side down, on covered grill over medium, indirect heat* about 30 to 35 minutes or until chicken is tender and juices run clear. Remove and discard skin. Serve chicken on buns topped with cheese, ham and Peach-Mint Salsa. Garnish with lettuce. Serve with Savory Grilled Peaches.

Makes 4 hearty sandwiches

Peach-Mint Salsa

1 fresh California peach, chopped (about 2/3 cup)
1/3 cup chopped green onions
1 tomato, chopped
1 1/2 tablespoons chopped fresh mint
1/4 teaspoon chili powder

In small bowl, combine all ingredients. Refrigerate leftovers.

Makes about 1 1/2 cups

Savory Grilled Peaches: Cut 4 fresh California peaches in half. Cook on covered grill over medium, indirect heat* 4 minutes. Turn; cook an additional 4 minutes or until heated through. Makes 4 servings.

Tip: Sandwiches are delicious served either hot or cold.

*See page 160 for information about indirect heat grilling method.

*Favorite recipe from **California Tree Fruit Agreement***

Lemon Herbed Chicken

1/2 cup butter or margarine
1/2 cup vegetable oil
1/3 cup lemon juice
2 tablespoons finely chopped fresh parsley
2 tablespoons garlic salt
1 teaspoon dried rosemary leaves, crushed
1 teaspoon dried summer savory leaves, crushed
1/2 teaspoon dried thyme leaves, crushed
1/4 teaspoon pepper
6 chicken breasts (about 4 1/2 pounds)

Combine all ingredients, except chicken, in saucepan. Heat over medium heat until butter melts. Arrange chicken in shallow glass dish; brush with sauce 10 to 15 minutes before cooking. Lightly oil grid. Grill chicken, skin side down, on uncovered grill, over medium-hot KINGSFORD® briquets, 45 to 60 minutes, turning and basting with sauce every 10 minutes, until fork-tender.

Makes 6 servings

Grilled Chicken, Corn & Avocado Salad

2 tablespoons lime juice
2 tablespoons vinegar
1 cup olive oil
1 small bunch cilantro, divided
1 clove garlic, peeled
2 green onions, cut into 1-inch
    pieces
  Salt and black pepper
6 ears fresh corn,* silk and husks
    intact
2 boneless chicken breasts, halved
    (about 1¼ pounds)
2 Anaheim or poblano peppers,*
    roasted, peeled and diced
1 large red bell pepper,* roasted,
    peeled and diced
2 large avocados, halved, peeled,
    pitted and diced
  Crisp salad greens

Pour lime juice and vinegar into blender or food processor container. While processing, slowly add oil in thin stream. Add ¾ of cilantro leaves; process until leaves are finely chopped. Add garlic, onions and salt and black pepper to taste; process until onions are chopped. Set dressing aside.

Roast corn in husks on covered grill over medium-hot** heat about 25 minutes or until tender. Cool slightly, then remove husks and silk. Cut corn from cobs; set aside.

Season chicken with salt and black pepper. Grill, skin side down, 8 minutes. Turn chicken over; cook 5 minutes or until chicken is tender and juices run clear. Keep warm.

Toss corn with roasted peppers, avocados and dressing in large bowl. Arrange chicken on serving plate lined with greens. Garnish with remaining cilantro. Serve with corn mixture.

Makes 4 servings

*Two cups frozen corn, cooked, 1 can (4 ounces) chopped green chilies, drained, and 1 jar (7 ounces) roasted red peppers, drained, may be substituted for the fresh corn and peppers.

**Coals are medium-hot when you can *cautiously* hold the palm of your hand 4 inches above the coals for a count of 3 seconds.

*Favorite recipe from **California Avocado Festival Cook-Off***

Cajun Chicken Burgers

1 pound fresh ground chicken
1 small onion, finely chopped
¼ cup chopped green or red bell
    pepper
3 green onions, minced
1 clove garlic, minced
1 teaspoon Worcestershire sauce
½ teaspoon TABASCO® Pepper Sauce
  Ground black pepper

In medium bowl, combine chicken, onion, bell pepper, onions, garlic, Worcestershire sauce, Tabasco® sauce and black pepper. Form chicken mixture into five 3-inch patties. Grill or broil patties 6 minutes; turn over. Grill an additional 4 to 6 minutes or until burgers are no longer pink in center and juices run clear. Serve immediately.

Makes 5 servings

Grilled Chicken, Corn & Avocado Salad

Spicy Orange Chicken

Spicy Orange Chicken

1 cup water
1 medium onion, chopped
1 can (6 ounces) frozen orange juice
    concentrate, thawed, undiluted
¼ cup catsup
3 medium cloves garlic, minced
1 teaspoon ground cinnamon
1 teaspoon TABASCO® Pepper Sauce
¼ teaspoon salt
2 broiler-fryer chickens, cut up
    (2½ to 3 pounds)

In medium bowl, combine water, onion, orange juice concentrate, catsup, garlic, cinnamon, Tabasco® sauce and salt; mix well. Place chicken in large, shallow dish or resealable plastic bag; add marinade. Cover; refrigerate at least 4 to 6 hours, turning chicken occasionally.

Remove chicken from marinade; place on grill 4 to 5 inches from heat. Grill 25 to 30 minutes or until chicken is tender and juices run clear; turn frequently, basting with marinade. Bring any remaining marinade to a boil over medium-high heat; boil 1 minute. Serve with chicken. Garnish as desired.

Makes 8 servings

Grilled Stuffed Chicken Breasts

3 boneless skinless chicken breasts,
   halved (about 2 pounds)
6 tablespoons butter or margarine
3 tablespoons Dijon-style mustard,
   divided
6 thin slices cooked ham
1 cup (4 ounces) shredded Swiss
   cheese
3 tablespoons vegetable oil
1 tablespoon honey
   Salt and pepper

Pound chicken breast halves to ¼-inch thickness. Blend butter with 2 tablespoons mustard; spread butter mixture over one side of each chicken breast half. Cut each ham slice to fit each chicken breast half; place on top of butter mixture. Top each with evenly divided portions of cheese. Roll chicken pieces; skewer each to enclose ham and cheese. Mix remaining 1 tablespoon mustard with oil and honey; brush over all sides of each chicken roll. Season chicken rolls with salt and pepper. Grill chicken, on covered grill, over medium-hot KINGSFORD® with Mesquite charcoal briquets, 25 to 35 minutes, basting often with mustard-honey mixture, until fork-tender.

Makes 6 servings

Barbecued Chicken Italiano

½ cup REALEMON® Lemon Juice
   from Concentrate
½ cup vegetable oil
1 teaspoon garlic salt
1 teaspoon oregano leaves
¼ teaspoon pepper
1 (2½- to 3-pound) broiler-fryer
   chicken, cut up

In plastic bag or shallow dish, combine ReaLemon® brand, oil, garlic salt, oregano and pepper; mix well. Add chicken; cover. Marinate in refrigerator 6 hours or overnight, turning occasionally. Remove chicken from marinade; heat marinade thoroughly. Grill or broil chicken as desired, turning and basting frequently with marinade. Refrigerate leftovers.

Makes 4 to 6 servings

Chicken Teriyaki Kabobs

2 boneless skinless chicken breasts,
   cut into 1½-inch cubes (about
   1¼ pounds)
1 bunch green onions, cut into
   1-inch lengths
½ cup KIKKOMAN® Soy Sauce
2 tablespoons sugar
1 teaspoon vegetable oil
1 teaspoon minced fresh ginger root
1 clove garlic, minced

Thread each of eight 6-inch bamboo or metal skewers alternately with chicken and green onion pieces. (Spear green onion pieces through sides.) Place skewers in shallow pan. Combine soy sauce, sugar, oil, ginger and garlic. Pour marinade over kabobs; brush chicken thoroughly with sauce. Marinate 30 minutes. Reserving marinade, remove kabobs and place on grill. Grill 3 minutes; turn over and brush with reserved marinade. Grill 3 minutes longer, or until chicken is tender.

Makes 4 servings

Ranch Chicken

⅓ cup vegetable oil
¾ cup apple juice
¼ cup wine vinegar
1 package (1 ounce)
    HIDDEN VALLEY RANCH®
    Milk Recipe Original Ranch®
    Salad Dressing Mix
2 tablespoons soy sauce
½ teaspoon pepper
3 fresh kiwifruit, peeled, divided
4 boneless skinless chicken breasts,
    halved (about 2½ pounds)
6 cups hot cooked wild or white rice

In blender or food processor container, process oil, apple juice, vinegar, salad dressing mix, soy sauce and pepper on high speed 1 minute. Add 2 kiwifruit; process until smooth. Pour 1 cup marinade over chicken; reserve remaining marinade. Marinate chicken 20 minutes. Remove chicken; discard marinade. Grill or broil chicken 4 to 6 minutes on each side until tender and juices run clear. Remove from heat; slice into strips. Slice remaining kiwifruit. Place chicken strips over rice; top with kiwifruit slices. Serve with reserved marinade.   *Serves 6 as a main dish*

Sesame Grilled Chicken

½ cup white wine
⅓ cup white vinegar
1 tablespoon sesame oil
⅓ cup vegetable oil
2 cloves garlic, sliced
1 tablespoon chopped fresh ginger
2 sprigs fresh thyme *or* ¼ teaspoon
    dried thyme leaves
1 tablespoon sesame seed
1 broiler-fryer chicken, quartered
    (2 to 3 pounds)

Combine all ingredients, except chicken, in small bowl. Rinse chicken with cold water; pat dry with paper towels. Arrange chicken in glass baking dish. Pour marinade over chicken. Cover; marinate about 3 hours or up to 24 hours in refrigerator. Drain chicken; reserve marinade. Grill chicken quarters, skin side down, on covered grill, over medium-hot KINGSFORD® briquets, 15 to 20 minutes, brushing often with heated reserved marinade. Turn chicken over; cook about 20 minutes, brushing often with marinade, until chicken is fork-tender.
Makes 4 servings

Lemon Honey Chicken

¼ cup CRISCO® Oil
1 teaspoon grated lemon peel
6 tablespoons lemon juice
2 tablespoons honey
    Dash salt and pepper
6 chicken pieces

1. Combine Crisco® Oil, lemon peel, lemon juice, honey, salt and pepper in glass baking dish. Stir well.

2. Place chicken pieces in baking dish. Turn to coat. Marinate at room temperature 20 minutes.

3. Preheat grill.* Remove chicken from marinade, reserving marinade.

4. Grill chicken 15 to 20 minutes. Brush with marinade. Grill on other side 15 to 20 minutes or until juices run clear and meat near bone is no longer pink.
Makes 4 to 6 servings

*Broiler may also be used.

Chicken Kabobs
in Pita Bread

¼ cup olive or vegetable oil
¼ cup lemon juice
½ teaspoon salt
½ teaspoon dried oregano leaves
¼ teaspoon garlic powder
⅛ teaspoon pepper
1 boneless skinless chicken breast,
    cut into 1-inch cubes (about
    10 ounces)
2 large pita breads
1 small onion, thinly sliced
1 tomato, thinly sliced
½ cup plain yogurt
    Fresh parsley sprigs (optional)

Mix oil, lemon juice, salt, oregano,
garlic powder and pepper in medium
glass bowl. Add chicken; toss to coat
completely. Cover and refrigerate at
least 3 hours or overnight.

Remove chicken from marinade,
reserving marinade. Thread chicken
onto 4 small metal skewers. Place
kabobs on greased grill. Cook about
5 inches from heat until chicken is
browned, 8 to 10 minutes, brushing
often with reserved marinade. Turn
kabobs over; brush with marinade. Grill
until chicken is tender and no longer
pink, 5 to 7 minutes.

Cut each pita bread in half; gently pull
each half open to form a pocket. For
each sandwich, remove chicken from
1 skewer and place inside 1 pita bread
half; top with onion, tomato and
yogurt. Garnish with parsley. Serve hot.
Makes 4 servings

Chicken Kabobs in Pita Bread

Southern Barbecued
Chicken

⅔ cup HEINZ® Tomato Ketchup
1 tablespoon honey
2 teaspoons lemon juice
    Dash hot pepper sauce
1 broiler-fryer chicken, cut up
    (2 to 2½ pounds)

In small bowl, combine ketchup, honey,
lemon juice and hot pepper sauce. Grill
or broil chicken 25 to 30 minutes, turning
once. Brush ketchup mixture on chicken;
cook additional 5 to 10 minutes or until
chicken is tender and juices run clear,
brushing occasionally with ketchup
mixture.

Makes 4 to 5 servings (about ¾ cup sauce)

Marinated Lemon Chicken with Lemon-Pepper Noodles

⅓ cup olive or vegetable oil
⅓ cup lemon juice
 1 medium onion, sliced
 2 large cloves garlic, finely chopped
 1 tablespoon plus 1½ teaspoons grated lemon peel
 1 teaspoon parsley flakes
½ teaspoon dried oregano leaves
½ teaspoon salt
¼ teaspoon pepper
1½ pounds boneless skinless chicken breasts, halved
 1 package LIPTON® Noodles & Sauce – Butter & Herb
 Pepper

In large, shallow glass baking dish, combine oil, lemon juice, onion, garlic, 1 tablespoon lemon peel, parsley, oregano, salt and ¼ teaspoon pepper. Add chicken. Cover; marinate in refrigerator, stirring occasionally, at least 1 hour. Remove chicken and onion; discard marinade.

Grill or broil chicken with onion until chicken is tender and juices run clear. Meanwhile, prepare noodles & butter & herb sauce according to package directions. Stir in remaining 1½ teaspoons lemon peel; season with pepper to taste. To serve, arrange chicken and onion over noodles. Garnish as desired.   *Makes 4 servings*

Marinated Lemon Chicken with Lemon-Pepper Noodles

Grilled Italian Chicken

½ cup prepared HIDDEN VALLEY RANCH® Ranch Italian Salad Dressing
 1 tablespoon Dijon-style mustard
 2 boneless skinless chicken breasts, halved (about 1¼ pounds)

In small bowl or measuring cup, whisk together salad dressing and mustard; reserve 3 tablespoons. Brush chicken generously with some of the remaining dressing mixture. Grill or broil, basting several times with dressing mixture, until chicken is golden and tender, about 5 minutes on each side. Brush chicken generously with reserved 3 tablespoons dressing mixture just before removing from grill; serve hot.
Serves 4 as a main dish

Grilled Deviled Chicken

¼ cup ketchup
¼ cup CRISCO® Oil
 2 tablespoons lemon juice
 1 tablespoon chili powder
 1 teaspoon lemon pepper seasoning
½ teaspoon ground oregano
½ teaspoon onion powder
⅛ teaspoon ground red pepper
 1 broiler-fryer chicken, cut up (2½ to 3 pounds)

1. Combine all ingredients, except chicken, in small bowl. Mix well. Set aside.

2. Place chicken on greased grill over medium coals. Grill, turning over frequently, 45 to 60 minutes or until juices run clear and meat near bone is no longer pink. Brush with sauce during last 15 minutes of grilling.
Makes 4 servings

Crisp 'n' Savory Grilled Chicken

Herb-Marinated Chicken Kabobs

**2 boneless skinless chicken breasts,
  halved (about 1¼ pounds)**
**2 small zucchini, cut into ½-inch
  slices**
**1 large red bell pepper, cut into
  1-inch squares**
**½ cup HEINZ® Gourmet Wine
  Vinegar**
½ cup tomato juice
2 tablespoons vegetable oil
1 tablespoon chopped onion
1 tablespoon brown sugar
2 cloves garlic, minced
½ teaspoon dried oregano leaves
½ teaspoon black pepper

Lightly flatten chicken breast halves; cut
each half lengthwise into 3 strips. In
large bowl, combine chicken, zucchini
and red pepper. For marinade, in jar,
combine remaining ingredients; cover
and shake vigorously. Pour marinade
over chicken and vegetables. Cover;
marinate in refrigerator about 1 hour.
Drain chicken and vegetables, reserving
marinade. Alternately thread chicken
and vegetables onto skewers; brush
with marinade. Grill or broil kabobs, 3
to 5 inches from heat, 8 to 10 minutes
or until chicken is tender and no longer
pink in center, turning and brushing
occasionally with marinade.

Makes 4 servings

Crisp 'n' Savory Grilled Chicken

¼ cup margarine or butter
**½ cup REALEMON® Lemon Juice
  from Concentrate**
½ cup water
4 teaspoons soy sauce
1 tablespoon salt
**1 (2½- to 3-pound) broiler-fryer
  chicken, cut up**

In small saucepan, melt margarine; stir
in ReaLemon® brand, water, soy sauce
and salt. Grill or broil chicken as
desired, turning and basting frequently
with sauce. Refrigerate leftovers.

Makes 4 to 6 servings

Cool Grilled Chicken Salad

    1 pound boneless skinless chicken
        breasts
    ¼ cup lemon juice
    2 tablespoons olive or vegetable oil
    1 teaspoon dried tarragon leaves,
        crushed
    ¾ teaspoon LAWRY'S® Garlic Salt
    1 quart salad greens, torn into bite-
        size pieces
    6 medium red potatoes, cooked,
        cooled and cut into chunks
    1 cup shredded carrot
      Last Minute Dressing (recipe
        follows)

Rinse chicken and place in resealable plastic bag. In small bowl, combine lemon juice, oil, tarragon and Garlic Salt; blend well. Pour marinade over chicken; seal bag and refrigerate 30 to 45 minutes or overnight. Remove chicken; reserve marinade. Grill or broil chicken 4 minutes on each side, basting with heated reserved marinade, until chicken is golden and tender. Cool; cut into strips. Line individual plates with salad greens. Arrange potato chunks, carrot and chicken on top.

Makes 6 side-dish or 4 main-dish servings

Last Minute Dressing

    ⅔ cup vegetable oil
    ¼ cup white wine vinegar
    1½ tablespoons Dijon-style mustard
    1 tablespoon water
    2 teaspoons sugar
    1 teaspoon LAWRY'S® Seasoned Salt
    ½ teaspoon LAWRY'S® Lemon
        Pepper Seasoning

In medium bowl, blender or food processor container, combine all ingredients; blend well with wire whisk or process 15 seconds.　　*Makes 1 cup*

Hint: For a more colorful salad, add sliced tomatoes or shredded red cabbage.

Oriental Grilled Chicken

    1 broiler-fryer chicken, quartered
        (2 to 3 pounds)*
    2 tablespoons prepared mustard
    ¼ cup soy sauce
    4 teaspoons honey
    1 tablespoon lemon juice
    ¼ teaspoon ground ginger

In medium bowl, combine mustard and soy sauce. Gradually stir in honey; add lemon juice and ginger. Place chicken in shallow glass dish. Pour marinade over chicken; cover and refrigerate about 1 hour. Drain chicken; reserve marinade. Grill chicken, skin side up, on covered grill, over medium-hot Kingsford® briquets, about 45 minutes to 1 hour, until fork-tender. Baste with marinade during last 15 minutes of grilling.

Makes 4 servings

*16 broiler-fryer chicken wings may be used instead of chicken quarters. Reduce grilling time to about 30 minutes.

*Favorite recipe from **National Broiler Council***

Kansas City-Style Barbecued Chicken Legs

1/2 cup butter or margarine, softened
1/3 cup finely chopped fresh parsley
2 cloves garlic, minced
12 chicken legs (2¾ to 3 pounds)
    Olive or vegetable oil
    K.C. MASTERPIECE® Barbecue
    Sauce

Blend butter, parsley and garlic in small bowl. Rinse chicken legs with cold water; pat dry with paper towels. Starting at thick end of each leg, work finger between skin and meat to form a pocket. Insert about 2 teaspoons butter mixture into each pocket; massage outer skin to spread filling. Rub completed legs with 3 tablespoons oil.

Lightly oil grid. Grill chicken, on covered grill, over medium-hot KINGSFORD® briquets, about 45 minutes or until fork-tender. Turn and baste occasionally with additional oil. About 15 minutes before chicken is finished grilling, baste thoroughly with 3/4 cup barbecue sauce. Baste once more before serving. Serve with additional warmed barbecue sauce, if desired.

Makes 6 servings

Lemon Chicken Grill

1/4 cup fresh lemon juice
1 can (4 ounces) chopped green
    chilies
3 tablespoons olive or vegetable oil
3/4 teaspoon LAWRY'S® Lemon
    Pepper Seasoning
1/2 teaspoon LAWRY'S® Garlic Powder
    with Parsley
1/2 teaspoon LAWRY'S® Seasoned Salt
1½ pounds chicken breasts
    LAWRY'S® Seasoned Salt

In blender or food processor container, combine lemon juice, chilies, oil, Lemon Pepper Seasoning, Garlic Powder with Parsley and 1/2 teaspoon Seasoned Salt. Blend until smooth. Place chicken in glass dish; cover with marinade. Refrigerate, covered, at least 1 hour. Remove chicken; reserve marinade. Grill or broil chicken 20 to 25 minutes, turning and basting often with marinade, until chicken is tender. Season with additional Seasoned Salt, if desired. *Makes 4 servings*

Presentation: Serve with coleslaw and warm flour tortillas.

Hint: Do not baste chicken with marinade during last 5 minutes of cooking.

Grilled Basil-Lime Chicken

1/2 cup lime juice (of 3 limes)
1/2 cup olive oil
1½ teaspoons dried basil leaves
3 cloves garlic, minced
1/4 teaspoon pepper
2 boneless skinless chicken breasts,
    halved (about 1¼ pounds)
1 tub (12 ounces) OCEAN SPRAY®
    Cran-Fruit™ Crushed Fruit for
    Chicken

Combine all ingredients, except chicken, and Cran-Fruit™ Crushed Fruit for Chicken in small bowl. Pour marinade into large, resealable plastic bag or nonmetal bowl. Pierce chicken breasts on both sides with fork. Cover; marinate 1 hour in refrigerator, turning frequently. Remove chicken; reserve marinade. Grill chicken until tender and juices run clear, brushing frequently with reserved marinade. Serve with Cran-Fruit™ Crushed Fruit for Chicken.

Makes 4 servings

Grilled Curried Chicken

**1 cup (8 ounces) WISH-BONE®
  Blended Italian Dressing**
**½ cup finely ground unsalted
  peanuts**
½ cup orange marmalade
2 teaspoons curry powder
½ teaspoon dried tarragon leaves
**2 boneless skinless chicken breasts,
  halved (about 1¼ pounds)**

In large, shallow baking dish, combine
all ingredients except chicken. Add
chicken; turn to coat. Cover; marinate
in refrigerator, turning occasionally, 4
hours or overnight. Remove chicken;
reserve marinade.

Grill or broil chicken, turning and
basting frequently with reserved
marinade, until chicken is tender and
juices run clear. If chicken browns too
quickly, cover loosely with aluminum
foil.   *Makes 4 servings*

•Also terrific with Wish-Bone® Creamy
Italian or Lite Creamy Italian Dressing.

Chicken and Fruit Kabobs

1¾ cups honey
¾ cup fresh lemon juice
½ cup Dijon-style mustard
⅓ cup chopped fresh ginger
**4 pounds boneless skinless chicken
  breasts, cut up**
6 fresh plums, pitted and quartered
3 firm bananas, cut into chunks
**4 cups fresh pineapple chunks
  (about half of medium
  pineapple)**

Chicken and Fruit Kabobs

Combine honey, lemon juice, mustard
and ginger in small bowl; mix well.
Thread chicken and fruit onto skewers,
alternating chicken with fruit; brush
generously with honey mixture. Place
kabobs on grill about 4 inches from
heat. Grill 5 minutes on each side,
brushing frequently with honey
mixture. Grill 10 minutes or until
chicken is no longer pink in center,
turning and brushing frequently with
remaining honey mixture.

Makes 12 servings

COMPANY'S COMING

Special occasions call for special dishes. Chicken alla Vineyard or Almond Chicken Paprika are elegant entrées certain to make any gathering memorable.

Stuffed Chicken with Apple Glaze

1 broiler-fryer chicken (3½ to
    4 pounds)
½ teaspoon salt
¼ teaspoon pepper
2 tablespoons vegetable oil
1 package (6 ounces) chicken-
    flavored stuffing mix *plus*
    ingredients to prepare mix
1 cup chopped apple
¼ cup chopped walnuts
¼ cup raisins
¼ cup thinly sliced celery
½ teaspoon grated lemon peel
½ cup apple jelly
1 tablespoon lemon juice
½ teaspoon ground cinnamon

Preheat oven to 350°F. Sprinkle inside of chicken with salt and pepper; rub outside with oil. Prepare stuffing mix in large bowl according to package directions. Add apple, walnuts, raisins, celery and lemon peel; mix thoroughly. Stuff body cavity loosely with stuffing.* Place chicken in baking pan. Cover loosely with aluminum foil; roast 1 hour.

Meanwhile, combine jelly, lemon juice and cinnamon in small saucepan. Simmer over low heat 3 minutes or until blended. Remove foil from chicken; brush with jelly glaze. Roast chicken, uncovered, brushing frequently with jelly glaze, 30 minutes or until meat thermometer inserted into thickest part of thigh registers 185°F and juices run clear. Let chicken stand 15 minutes before carving. *Makes 4 servings*

*Bake any leftover stuffing in covered casserole alongside chicken until heated through.

Favorite recipe from **Delmarva Poultry Industry, Inc.**

Stuffed Chicken with Apple Glaze

Chicken in Lemon Sauce

Chicken in Lemon Sauce

4 boneless skinless chicken breasts,
   halved (about 2½ pounds)
¼ cup butter or margarine
2 tablespoons dry white wine
½ teaspoon grated lemon peel
2 tablespoons lemon juice
¼ teaspoon salt
⅛ teaspoon white pepper
1 cup heavy cream
1 cup sliced mushrooms
⅓ cup grated Parmesan cheese
   Red grapes and lemon peel for
   garnish

Melt butter in large skillet over medium heat; add chicken. Cook, turning, about 10 minutes or until browned and fork can be inserted into chicken with ease. Remove chicken to broiler-proof serving dish. Drain butter. Add wine, lemon peel and lemon juice to skillet; cook and stir over medium heat 1 minute. Stir in salt and pepper. Gradually pour in cream, stirring constantly, until hot. *Do not boil.* Pour cream sauce over chicken; sprinkle with mushrooms and cheese. Broil chicken, about 6 inches from heat, until lightly browned. Garnish with grapes and lemon peel.   *Makes 8 servings*

*Favorite recipe from **National Broiler Council***

Chicken Provençal with Mushroom Wild Rice

3 boneless skinless chicken breasts, halved (about 2 pounds)
1 tablespoon olive oil
1/2 teaspoon salt
1/4 teaspoon freshly ground black pepper
2 cloves garlic, minced
1 can (14 to 16 ounces) Italian plum tomatoes, drained and chopped
1/4 cup dry red wine
1 tablespoon capers, rinsed and drained
1 teaspoon dried thyme leaves, crushed
2 cups quartered mushrooms
2 tablespoons butter or margarine
2 cups water
1 package (6 1/4 ounces) UNCLE BEN'S® Original Fast Cooking Long Grain & Wild Rice
1/2 cup sliced green onions with tops

Pound chicken to 1/2-inch thickness. Cook chicken in oil in 12-inch skillet over medium-high heat until lightly browned, about 1 minute on each side. Sprinkle with salt and pepper. Add garlic to skillet; cook 1 minute. Add tomatoes, wine, capers and thyme; stir. Cover; simmer over low heat until chicken is tender and juices run clear, about 3 minutes.

Meanwhile, cook mushrooms in butter in medium saucepan over medium-high heat until lightly browned. Add water and contents of rice and seasoning packets to saucepan; bring to a vigorous boil. Reduce heat. Cover tightly; simmer until all water is absorbed, about 5 minutes. Remove chicken to serving platter. Cook tomato mixture over high heat to desired consistency. Spoon over chicken. Stir green onions into rice; serve with chicken.   *Makes 6 servings*

Boursin Baked Chicken

2 boneless chicken breasts, halved (about 1 1/4 pounds)
1/2 cup milk
2 cups plain dry bread crumbs
1/4 cup butter or margarine, melted
2 packages (4 ounces each) Boursin cheese, softened
Minced fresh parsley
1 tub (12 ounces) OCEAN SPRAY® Cran-Fruit™ Crushed Fruit for Chicken

Preheat oven to 350°F. Dip chicken in milk; roll in crumbs, coating evenly. Place chicken in single layer in baking pan. Drizzle butter over chicken. Bake 30 minutes or until chicken is tender and juices run clear. Remove chicken from oven. Carefully spread 1/4 cup cheese onto each breast. Sprinkle with parsley. Return chicken to oven; bake until cheese begins to melt, about 2 minutes. Serve with Cran-Fruit™ Crushed Fruit for Chicken.

Makes 4 servings

Curried Chicken Rolls

2 boneless skinless chicken breasts, halved (about 1¼ pounds)
½ teaspoon salt
⅛ teaspoon pepper
1 tablespoon butter or margarine
½ medium onion, finely chopped
¾ cup cooked rice
¼ cup raisins
1 tablespoon chopped fresh parsley
1 teaspoon curry powder
1 teaspoon brown sugar
½ teaspoon poultry seasoning
Pinch garlic powder
1 tablespoon vegetable oil
½ cup dry white wine
1 teaspoon instant chicken bouillon granules

Pound chicken breasts between 2 pieces of plastic wrap to ⅜-inch thickness; sprinkle with salt and pepper. Melt butter in medium skillet over medium heat. Add onion; cook and stir about 3 minutes or until tender. Remove from heat. Add rice, raisins, parsley, curry powder, brown sugar, poultry seasoning and garlic powder; mix well. Divide rice mixture into 4 equal portions. Spoon 1 portion onto half of each chicken breast half. Roll up chicken jelly-roll fashion; secure with wooden toothpicks.

Heat oil in large skillet over medium heat; add chicken rolls. Cook about 15 minutes or until browned on all sides. Add wine and bouillon. Cover; simmer 30 minutes or until fork can be inserted into chicken with ease. Garnish as desired.   *Makes 4 servings*

Serving Suggestion: Additional rice stuffing may be prepared and served alongside chicken rolls. Bake extra stuffing in covered casserole at 350°F until heated through.

*Favorite recipe from **National Broiler Council***

Champagne Chicken Valencia

½ cup all-purpose flour
½ teaspoon salt, divided
½ teaspoon pepper, divided
3 boneless skinless chicken breasts, halved (about 2 pounds)
¼ cup butter
¼ cup vegetable oil
1½ cups dry champagne or white wine
1 cup Florida orange juice
1 cup heavy cream
4 Florida Valencia oranges, peeled and sectioned*

Preheat oven to 350°F. In small bowl, mix flour with ¼ teaspoon salt and ¼ teaspoon pepper; coat chicken evenly with flour mixture.

In large skillet over medium-high heat, heat butter and oil; cook chicken until golden brown. Remove from skillet; arrange on baking sheet. Bake 20 minutes or until chicken is tender and juices run clear.

Meanwhile, drain fat from skillet. Add champagne, orange juice, remaining ¼ teaspoon salt and remaining ¼ teaspoon pepper; bring to a boil. Add cream; cook over high heat until sauce is reduced to about 2 cups.

Place chicken on heated serving platter; top with sauce. Garnish with orange sections.   *Makes 6 servings*

*Substitute any in-season orange if Valencia oranges are unavailable.

*Favorite recipe from **Florida Department of Citrus***

Curried Chicken Roll

Pineapple Chicken Madeira

Pineapple Chicken Madeira

1 can (8 ounces) DOLE® Pineapple
    Slices, undrained
1 boneless skinless chicken breast,
    halved (about 10 ounces)
2 tablespoons all-purpose flour
    Salt to taste
2 tablespoons margarine
¹/₂ cup julienne-cut DOLE® Red Bell
    Pepper
2 DOLE® Green Onions, sliced
3 tablespoons Madeira wine or
    sherry
¹/₂ cup cream

- Drain pineapple; reserve 2 tablespoons juice.
- Pound chicken to ¹/₂-inch thickness. Dredge chicken in flour seasoned with salt.
- In skillet over medium-high heat, sauté chicken in margarine on each side until lightly browned, about 3 minutes. Add reserved juice, red pepper, green onions and wine to skillet. Simmer 5 minutes or until chicken is tender and juices run clear.
- Remove chicken to serving platter. Stir cream into pan juices. Cook until liquid is reduced, about 1 minute; add pineapple and heat through. Top chicken with pineapple and sauce.

Makes 2 servings

Herb-Roasted Chicken

1 broiler-fryer chicken (2¹/₂ to
    3 pounds)
2 cloves garlic, quartered
¹/₄ cup CRISCO® Oil
1 tablespoon lime juice
1 teaspoon dried tarragon leaves
1 teaspoon dried chervil leaves
¹/₂ teaspoon dried thyme leaves
    Pepper

1. Preheat oven to 375°F. At neck cavity, lift skin of chicken from meat along breast, thigh and drumstick. Work finger between skin and meat to form pockets. Insert 6 pieces garlic between skin and breast meat. Cut small slit in each drumstick. Insert a piece of garlic into each slit.

2. Blend Crisco® Oil and lime juice in small bowl. Brush some of lime juice mixture on chicken. Mix tarragon, chervil and thyme in another small bowl. Rub onto chicken. Sprinkle chicken with pepper.

3. Place chicken, breast side up, in roasting pan. Bake at 375°F, 1¹/₄ to 1¹/₂ hours or until juices run clear and meat near the bone is no longer pink, brushing with remaining lime juice mixture several times during roasting. Let chicken stand 10 minutes before carving. *Makes 4 servings*

Buffet Chicken Medley

4 boneless skinless chicken breasts,
   quartered (about 2¹/₂ pounds)
2 tablespoons butter or margarine
1 large onion, cut into ¹/₄-inch
   chunks
1 jar (6 ounces) marinated artichoke
   hearts, sliced, marinade reserved
4 tomatoes, cut into wedges
1 teaspoon salt, divided
¹/₂ teaspoon pepper, divided
1 avocado, halved, peeled, pitted
   and cut into ¹/₂-inch wedges
4 ounces feta cheese, crumbled
   (about ¹/₂ cup)

In 10-inch skillet, melt butter over
medium-high heat. Add chicken pieces;
cook, turning, about 5 minutes or until
lightly browned. Remove chicken to
warm dish.

To pan drippings, add onion; cook over
medium heat 3 minutes, stirring
frequently. Add artichokes, marinade
and tomatoes; cook about 2 minutes.
Remove from heat. In 2-quart baking
dish, place half of chicken; sprinkle
with ¹/₂ teaspoon salt and ¹/₄ teaspoon
pepper. Spoon half of artichoke mixture
over chicken; add half of avocado and
half of cheese. Top with remaining
chicken; repeat layers. Bake at 350°F
about 25 minutes or until fork can be
inserted into chicken with ease.

Makes 8 servings

Favorite recipe from **National Broiler Council**

Buffet Chicken Medley

Chicken with Cucumbers and Dill

**2 boneless skinless chicken breasts,
  halved (about 1¼ pounds)**
1 teaspoon salt, divided
¾ teaspoon pepper, divided
**4 tablespoons butter or margarine,
  divided**
**2 cucumbers, peeled, seeded and cut
  into ¼-inch slices**
½ teaspoon dried dill weed
**¼ cup lemon juice
  Lemon slices, quartered, for
  garnish**

Sprinkle chicken breasts with
½ teaspoon salt and ½ teaspoon
pepper. Melt 2 tablespoons butter in
large skillet over medium heat; add
chicken. Cook about 8 minutes or until
chicken is browned on both sides.
Remove chicken from skillet; keep
warm. Remove and reserve pan juices.
Melt remaining 2 tablespoons butter in
same skillet. Add cucumbers; stir to
coat. Sprinkle remaining ½ teaspoon
salt and remaining ¼ teaspoon pepper
over cucumbers; cook 2 minutes. Stir in
dill. Push cucumbers to side of skillet.

Return chicken and reserved pan juices
to skillet. Cook 2 minutes or until
chicken is tender and juices run clear.
Place chicken on serving platter;
arrange cucumbers around chicken.
Cook juices in skillet until light brown.
Pour lemon juice and pan juices over
chicken. Garnish with lemon slices.

Makes 4 servings

*Favorite recipe from **Delmarva Poultry Industry, Inc.***

Chicken and Pasta in Cream Sauce

⅓ pound uncooked thin spaghetti
6 tablespoons unsalted butter
**1 tablespoon Chef Paul
  Prudhomme's
  POULTRY MAGIC®**
**½ pound boneless skinless chicken
  breast, diced**
¼ cup finely chopped green onions
2 cups heavy cream or half-and-half

Cook spaghetti according to package
directions to *al dente* stage. Drain
immediately; rinse with hot water to
wash off starch, then rinse with cold
water to stop cooking process. Drain
again. To prevent pasta from sticking
together, pour small amount of oil in
palm of hand and rub through pasta.

In large skillet, melt butter over
medium heat. Add Poultry Magic® and
chicken; sauté about 1 minute, stirring
occasionally. Add onions; sauté 1 to
2 minutes, continuing to stir. Gradually
add cream, shaking pan in back-and-
forth motion or stirring until mixture
boils. Reduce heat. Simmer until sauce
thickens slightly, continuing to shake
pan, 2 to 3 minutes. Add hot cooked
spaghetti; toss and stir until spaghetti is
heated through, about 2 minutes. Serve
immediately.

Makes 2 main-dish or 4 side-dish servings

Chicken with Cucumbers and Dill

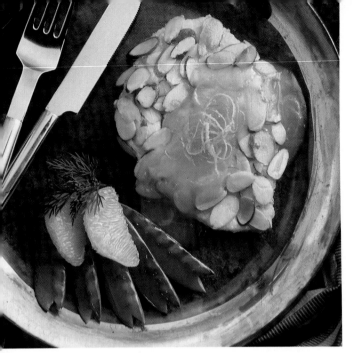

Almond Butter Chicken

Almond Butter Chicken

2 boneless skinless chicken breasts, halved (about 1¼ pounds)
2 tablespoons all-purpose flour
½ teaspoon salt
½ teaspoon pepper
1 egg, beaten
1 package (2¼ ounces) sliced almonds
¼ cup butter
Orange Sauce (recipe follows)

Place each chicken breast half between 2 pieces of plastic wrap. Pound to ¼-inch thickness. Coat chicken with flour. Sprinkle with salt and pepper. Dip one side of each chicken breast into egg; press with almonds. Melt butter in large skillet over medium high heat. Cook chicken, almond side down, 3 to 5 minutes or until almonds are toasted; turn chicken over. Reduce heat to medium-low; cook 10 to 12 minutes or until chicken is tender and juices run clear. Serve, almond side up, with Orange Sauce. Garnish as desired.

Makes 4 servings

Orange Sauce

1 tablespoon brown sugar
2 teaspoons cornstarch
  Juice of 1 orange (about ½ cup)
2 tablespoons butter
1 teaspoon grated orange peel

Combine brown sugar and cornstarch in saucepan. Add juice, butter and peel. Cook over medium heat, stirring constantly, until thickened.

Makes ⅔ cup

Favorite recipe from **Wisconsin Milk Marketing Board** *© 1992*

Chicken and Rice en Croute

1 package (10 ounces) refrigerated pizza dough
1 package (12 ounces) OCEAN SPRAY® Cran-Fruit™ Sauce, any flavor
2 boneless chicken breasts, halved, cooked (about 1¼ pounds)
1 cup cooked long-grain and wild rice*

Preheat oven to 350°F. Lightly grease cookie sheet. Unroll dough; cut in half crosswise, making two 8-inch squares. Slightly drain Cran-Fruit™ Sauce, if necessary.

Place dough on prepared cookie sheet. In center of each square, place 2 chicken breast halves, ½ cup rice and ½ package Cran-Fruit™ Sauce. Bring two opposite sides of square to center; firmly pinch dough together to seal. Seal ends. Bake 30 minutes or until dough is golden brown. Cut into pieces to serve.

Makes 4 servings

*Substitute 1 cup prepared stuffing for the rice.

Roast Chicken & Kiwifruit with Raspberry Glaze

2 broiler-fryer chickens, halved
(3½ to 4 pounds each)
1 teaspoon salt
¼ teaspoon pepper
¼ cup butter or margarine, melted
Raspberry Glaze (recipe follows)
2 kiwifruit, peeled and sliced

Preheat oven to 400°F. Sprinkle chicken with salt and pepper. Place, skin side up, in single layer in large, shallow pan; brush with butter. Roast, basting frequently with butter, about 45 minutes or until chicken is tender and juices run clear. Drain off fat. While chicken is roasting, prepare Raspberry Glaze. Spoon glaze over chicken; top with kiwifruit slices. Spoon glaze from bottom of pan over chicken and kiwifruit. Bake about 3 minutes or until kiwifruit and chicken are well glazed.

Makes 4 servings

Raspberry Glaze: Combine 1 cup seedless raspberry preserves, ½ cup white port wine and grated peel of 1 lemon in small saucepan. Cook over low heat about 5 minutes or until slightly thickened.

Favorite recipe from **Delmarva Poultry Industry, Inc.**

Roast Chicken & Kiwifruit with Raspberry Glaze

Chicken and Broccoli Crêpes

10 prepared Basic Crêpes (recipe follows)
½ cup half-and-half
½ cup all-purpose flour
½ teaspoon garlic salt
1¼ cups chicken broth
2 cups (8 ounces) shredded Wisconsin Cheddar cheese, divided
½ cup (2 ounces) shredded Wisconsin Monterey Jack cheese
1½ cups dairy sour cream, divided
2 tablespoons diced pimiento
1 tablespoon parsley flakes
1 teaspoon paprika
1 can (4 ounces) sliced mushrooms, drained
2 tablespoons butter
2 packages (10 ounces each) frozen broccoli spears, cooked and drained
2 cups cubed cooked chicken

Prepare Basic Crêpes; set aside. Combine half-and-half, flour and garlic salt in medium saucepan; beat with wire whisk until smooth. Blend in chicken broth. Stir in 1 cup Cheddar cheese, Monterey Jack cheese, ½ cup sour cream, pimiento, parsley and paprika. Cook sauce over medium-low heat until mixture thickens, stirring constantly. Remove from heat; set aside. Melt butter in small skillet over medium-high heat. Cook and stir mushrooms in butter.

On half of each crêpe, place equally divided portions of cooked broccoli, chicken and mushrooms. Spoon 1 to 2 tablespoons cheese sauce over each.

Fold crêpes. Place in large, shallow baking dish. Pour remaining cheese sauce over crêpes. Top with remaining 1 cup sour cream and 1 cup Cheddar cheese. Bake, uncovered, in preheated 350°F oven 5 to 10 minutes or until cheese melts. Garnish with chopped fresh parsley, if desired.

Makes 10 crêpes

Basic Crêpes

3 eggs
½ teaspoon salt
2 cups plus 2 tablespoons all-purpose flour
Milk
¼ cup melted butter

Beat eggs and salt together in medium bowl with electric mixer or wire whisk. Add flour alternately with 2 cups milk, beating until smooth. Stir in melted butter.

Allow crêpe batter to stand 1 hour or more in refrigerator before cooking. The flour may expand and bubbles will collapse. The batter should be the consistency of heavy cream. If the batter is too thick, add 1 to 2 tablespoons additional milk and stir well.

Cook crêpes in heated, nonstick pan over medium-high heat. With one hand, pour 3 tablespoons batter into pan; with other hand, lift pan off heat. Quickly rotate pan until batter covers bottom; return pan to heat. Cook until light brown; turn and brown other side for a few seconds. *Makes about 30 crêpes*

Note: To store crêpes, separate with pieces of waxed paper and wrap air-tight. They may be frozen for up to 3 months.

*Favorite recipe from **Wisconsin Milk Marketing Board** © 1992*

Chicken and Broccoli Crêpes

Savory Orange Chicken

2 pounds chicken pieces
   Pepper
2 tablespoons vegetable oil
1 teaspoon finely chopped garlic
½ cup orange juice
½ cup dry white wine
1 teaspoon grated orange peel
   (optional)
1 cup water
1 envelope LIPTON® Rice &
   Sauce – Chicken Flavor
1 cup sliced mushrooms

Trim excess fat from chicken pieces; season with pepper.

In large skillet, heat oil over medium heat; cook garlic 30 seconds. Increase heat to medium-high. Add chicken; cook until browned. Drain. Add orange juice, wine and orange peel. Simmer, covered, stirring occasionally, 20 minutes or until chicken is tender and juices run clear; remove chicken. Into skillet, stir water, rice & chicken flavor sauce and mushrooms; bring to a boil. Reduce heat; simmer, stirring occasionally, 7 minutes or until rice is tender and sauce is desired consistency. Add chicken; heat through. Garnish with orange slices and finely chopped parsley, if desired. *Makes 4 servings*

Microwave Directions: Trim and season as directed. In 2-quart microwave-safe dish, arrange chicken, skin side down; cover with waxed paper. Microwave at HIGH 10 minutes, turning chicken once. Remove chicken; drain.

In same dish, microwave mushrooms with garlic, uncovered, at HIGH 1½ minutes, stirring once. Stir in orange juice, wine, water, orange peel and rice & chicken flavor sauce. Microwave, uncovered, at HIGH 5

minutes. Arrange chicken pieces on rice with thickest portions to outer edge of dish. Microwave, uncovered, at HIGH 7 minutes or until rice is done, chicken is tender and juices run clear. Garnish as directed.

Sweet Apricots and Roasted Chicken in Pasta

1 package (10 ounces) bow-tie
   noodles
1½ cups half-and-half
1 boneless skinless chicken breast,
   halved, roasted and sliced
   (about 10 ounces)
1 can (17 ounces) California apricot
   halves, drained and quartered
⅓ cup chopped green onions
2 tablespoons margarine
   Salt and pepper

Cook noodles according to package directions; drain. In medium saucepan over medium heat, simmer half-and-half 4 minutes. *Do not boil.* Add chicken, apricots, onions and margarine; simmer 2 minutes. Season with salt and pepper to taste. Pour over pasta; serve immediately. *Makes 4 servings*

Favorite recipe from **California Apricot Advisory Board**

Savory Orange Chicken

Almond Chicken with Onion

1 broiler-fryer chicken, cut up
    (2½ to 3½ pounds)
3 tablespoons vegetable oil
2 medium onions, halved, thinly
    sliced
3 cloves garlic, finely chopped
2 tablespoons chopped fresh cilantro
1 tablespoon chopped fresh thyme
    or 1 teaspoon dried thyme leaves
½ teaspoon salt
¼ teaspoon ground nutmeg
1 cup chicken stock or broth
⅓ cup amontillado sherry*
1 teaspoon lemon juice
¾ cup plus 1 tablespoon
       BLUE DIAMOND® Sliced
       Natural Almonds, toasted and
       divided**

Brown chicken in oil in large skillet over medium-high heat. Remove chicken from skillet; reserve. Pour off all but 1 tablespoon oil. Add onions and garlic; cook over low heat, stirring, until golden brown. Stir in cilantro, thyme, salt and nutmeg. Add reserved chicken and stock. Cover; cook 15 to 20 minutes or until chicken is tender and juices run clear. Remove chicken from skillet; keep warm. Stir in sherry; simmer sauce about 5 minutes or until sauce coats back of spoon. Add lemon juice and ¾ cup almonds. Pour sauce over chicken; sprinkle with remaining 1 tablespoon almonds.

Makes 4 servings

*Amontillado sherry has a dark, soft and nutty flavor. If amontillado sherry is unavailable, substitute dry sherry.

**See page 42 for directions for toasting almonds.

Chicken Breasts with Artichoke-Cheese Stuffing

4 boneless skinless chicken breasts,
    halved lengthwise (about
    2½ pounds)
1½ cups (6 ounces) shredded
       Monterey Jack cheese
¼ cup mayonnaise
1 tablespoon finely chopped onion
1 tablespoon parsley flakes
1 teaspoon Dijon-style mustard
1 jar (6 ounces) marinated artichoke
    hearts, drained
⅓ cup all-purpose flour
¼ teaspoon salt
⅛ teaspoon pepper
1 egg
2 tablespoons water
1 cup seasoned dry bread crumbs
⅓ cup CRISCO® Oil

1. Pound chicken breasts to ¼-inch thickness. Set aside. Mix cheese, mayonnaise, onion, parsley and mustard in small mixing bowl. Cut artichoke hearts into bite-size pieces. Stir into cheese mixture. Spread about ¼ cup cheese mixture in center of each piece of chicken. Roll up and secure ends with wooden toothpicks.

2. Mix flour, salt and pepper in shallow dish. Dip rolled chicken in flour mixture to coat. Set aside. Mix egg and water in shallow dish. Place crumbs in another shallow dish or on sheet of waxed paper. Dip rolled chicken in egg mixture; roll in crumbs, pressing to coat evenly. Cover; refrigerate coated chicken about 1 hour.

3. Preheat oven to 350°F. Place Crisco® Oil in 13×9-inch baking pan. Place in oven for 10 minutes. When hot, remove from oven. Using tongs, roll coated chicken in hot Crisco® Oil. Arrange chicken in pan. Bake at 350°F, 35 minutes or until chicken is tender and juices run clear. *Makes 8 servings*

Sierra Chicken Bundle

Sierra Chicken Bundles

**2 cups cooked Mexican or Spanish-
style rice mix**
¼ cup thinly sliced green onions
**½ teaspoon LAWRY'S® Seasoned
Pepper**
**4 boneless skinless chicken breasts
(about 2½ pounds)**
½ cup plain dry bread crumbs
¼ cup grated Parmesan cheese
½ teaspoon chili powder
½ teaspoon LAWRY'S® Garlic Salt
¼ teaspoon ground cumin
¼ cup margarine or butter, melted

In medium bowl, combine cooked rice
mix, green onions and Seasoned
Pepper. Pound chicken breasts between
2 sheets of waxed paper to ¼-inch
thickness. Place about ⅓ cup rice
mixture in center of each chicken
breast. Roll up each chicken breast,
tucking ends under; secure with
wooden skewers. In pie plate, combine
remaining ingredients except margarine;
blend well. Roll chicken bundles in
margarine, then in crumb mixture.
Place, seam side down, in 12×8-inch
baking dish. Bake, uncovered, in 400°F
oven 20 to 25 minutes or until chicken
is tender and juices run clear.

Makes 4 servings

Presentation: Serve with assorted
steamed vegetables and corn bread.

Apricot Chicken Oriental

1 tablespoon butter or margarine
2 boneless skinless chicken breasts,
    halved (about 1¼ pounds)
1 jar (10 ounces) apricot preserves
1 cup water
½ cup soy sauce
1 can (8 ounces) sliced water
    chestnuts, drained, liquid
    reserved
12 dried apricots, coarsely chopped
1 teaspoon ground ginger
1 teaspoon garlic powder
    Apricot Rice (recipe follows)
3 ribs celery, diagonally sliced
2 cups sliced mushrooms
1 bunch green onions, sliced
1 package (6 ounces) frozen pea
    pods
1 red or green bell pepper, cut into
    strips

Melt butter in large skillet over medium heat. Add chicken; brown evenly on both sides. Stir in preserves, water, soy sauce, liquid from water chestnuts, apricots, ginger and garlic powder. Simmer 40 minutes or until chicken is tender and juices run clear. Meanwhile, prepare Apricot Rice.

Add celery, mushrooms, onions, pea pods, red pepper and water chestnuts to skillet; cook and stir 5 minutes or until heated through. Serve chicken and vegetables over Apricot Rice. Garnish as desired.   *Makes 4 servings*

Apricot Rice: Combine 2½ cups water, ¼ cup finely chopped dried apricots and ¼ teaspoon salt in medium saucepan. Bring to a boil; stir in 1 cup long-grain rice. Reduce heat. Cover; simmer 20 minutes. Remove from heat; let stand 5 minutes.

Favorite recipe from California Apricot Advisory Board

Mexican Chicken Kiev

2 boneless skinless chicken breasts,
    halved and slightly pounded
    (about 1¼ pounds)
4 ounces Monterey Jack cheese,
    thinly sliced
1 can (4 ounces) chopped green
    chilies, drained
⅓ cup seasoned dry bread crumbs
1 teaspoon chili powder
    Prepared salsa

Preheat oven to 375°F. Top each chicken breast half with equal amounts of cheese and chilies. Roll up; secure with wooden toothpicks. Roll chicken in crumbs combined with chili powder to coat evenly.

In lightly greased, shallow baking pan, arrange chicken rolls; bake 20 minutes. Top with ½ cup salsa; bake 20 minutes or until chicken is tender and juices run clear. Serve with additional salsa, if desired.   *Makes 4 servings*

Microwave Directions: Assemble chicken rolls as directed. In lightly greased, 2-quart microwave-safe oblong baking dish, arrange chicken rolls. Microwave, covered with plastic wrap, at HIGH 5 minutes. Rearrange chicken; top with salsa. Microwave 3 minutes or until chicken is tender. Let stand, covered, 5 minutes. Serve as directed.

Favorite recipe from Thomas J. Lipton Co.

Apricot Chicken Oriental

Plum Sweet and Spicy Chicken

1 broiler-fryer chicken (3½ to
    4 pounds)
½ teaspoon white pepper
½ teaspoon ground ginger
½ teaspoon ground cinnamon
¼ teaspoon ground cloves
4 tablespoons soy sauce, divided
2 tablespoons honey
½ cup plum jelly
¼ cup chutney
2 teaspoons sugar
2 teaspoons vinegar

Combine pepper, ginger, cinnamon and cloves in small dish. Rub inside of chicken with half of spice mixture. Stir 1 tablespoon soy sauce into remaining spice mixture; rub onto outside of chicken. Cover chicken; refrigerate 1 hour.

Place chicken, breast side up, on rack in wok over 2 inches of boiling water. Cover; steam 1 hour, adding water to wok as needed.

Preheat oven to 350°F. Remove chicken to shallow baking pan. Bake about 15 minutes or until leg moves freely when twisted; remove from oven. *Increase oven temperature to 450°F.* Combine remaining 3 tablespoons soy sauce and honey; brush on chicken. Combine plum jelly, chutney, sugar and vinegar; spread on chicken. Bake 10 minutes or until chicken is tender and juices run clear. Let chicken stand 15 minutes before carving. Garnish as desired. *Makes 4 servings*

*Favorite recipe from **National Broiler Council***

Almond Chicken Paprika

1 cup BLUE DIAMOND® Whole
    Natural Almonds, toasted*
2 boneless skinless chicken breasts,
    halved (about 1¼ pounds)
  Salt
  Freshly ground white pepper
8 tablespoons butter, divided
2 teaspoons Dijon-style mustard
2½ tablespoons paprika, divided
  All-purpose flour
⅔ cup chopped onion
  Pinch ground red pepper
1 cup chicken stock or broth
½ cup sour cream

Coarsely chop almonds; place in shallow dish and reserve. Lightly flatten chicken breasts. Season with salt and white pepper. Melt 6 tablespoons butter in medium skillet. Whisk in mustard and 1 tablespoon paprika. Coat chicken in flour, then in mustard mixture. Roll in reserved almonds to coat evenly. Place chicken on buttered baking sheet. Bake at 450°F, 10 to 15 minutes or until chicken is tender and juices run clear.

Meanwhile, melt remaining 2 tablespoons butter in small saucepan. Add onion; cook and stir until translucent. Stir in remaining 1½ tablespoons paprika, 1 tablespoon flour, ½ teaspoon salt and ground red pepper. Cook 1 minute. Stir in chicken stock; simmer 5 minutes. Whisk in sour cream; heat through. *Do not boil.* Divide sauce among 4 individual plates; top each with one chicken breast half.
Makes 4 servings

*See page 42 for directions for toasting almonds.

Plum Sweet and Spicy Chicken

Corn Bread and Sausage Stuffed Chicken

3/4 cup chopped BLUE DIAMOND®
    Whole Natural Almonds
1 tablespoon butter
2 hot Italian sausage links
    (8 to 10 ounces)
1 small red onion, finely diced
2 cloves garlic, finely chopped
1 small rib celery, finely diced
3 cups crumbled corn bread
1/2 cup heavy cream
1/2 teaspoon salt
1/4 teaspoon freshly ground black
    pepper
1 broiler-fryer chicken (2 1/2 to
    3 1/2 pounds)

Cook and stir almonds in butter in large skillet over medium-high heat until crisp. Remove from skillet; reserve. Remove casing from sausage; cook and stir sausage until brown and crumbly. Add onion, garlic and celery; cook and stir until translucent. Remove skillet from heat. Add corn bread, cream and reserved almonds; mix thoroughly. Season with salt and pepper.

Cut chicken along each side of backbone to remove bone. (Reserve neck, giblets and liver for another use.) With heel of hand, smash breastbone to flatten. Carefully lift skin of chicken from meat along breasts, thighs and drumsticks. Work finger between skin and meat to form pockets. Stuff corn bread mixture into pockets. Cut slit into loose skin on each side of breastbone end. With drumsticks turned in toward body, insert drumstick tips into slits. Bake at 475°F, 10 minutes. *Reduce heat to* 350°F. Bake 30 minutes or until temperature on meat thermometer inserted into thigh registers 185°F and juices run clear. Let stand 10 minutes before serving. *Makes 4 servings*

Note: Whole chickens roast more quickly and are easier to carve when backbone is removed and breastbone is flattened.

Chicken Breasts in Wine Sauce

1/3 cup plus 2 tablespoons all-purpose
    flour, divided
1/2 teaspoon onion salt
1/4 teaspoon pepper
2 skinless chicken breasts, halved
    lengthwise (about 1 1/2 pounds)
3 tablespoons CRISCO® Oil
2 small onions, cut into thirds
2/3 cup dry white wine
1 teaspoon instant chicken bouillon
    granules
1/2 teaspoon dried tarragon leaves
3/4 cup half-and-half

1. Mix 1/3 cup flour, onion salt and pepper in large plastic bag. Add chicken. Shake to coat.

2. Heat Crisco® Oil in large skillet. Add chicken. Brown over medium-high heat. Add onions, wine, bouillon granules and tarragon. Heat to boiling. Cover. Reduce heat. Simmer about 20 minutes or until juices run clear and meat near bone is no longer pink. Transfer chicken to serving platter. Cover to keep warm. Remove and discard onions; reserve skillet drippings.

3. Place half-and-half in small bowl. Blend in remaining 2 tablespoons flour. Stir into skillet drippings. Cook over medium-low heat, stirring constantly, until thickened and bubbly. Serve with chicken. *Makes 4 servings*

Dressed Chicken Breasts with Angel Hair Pasta

1 cup prepared
   HIDDEN VALLEY RANCH®
   Original Ranch® Salad Dressing
¹/₃ cup Dijon-style mustard
4 boneless skinless chicken breasts,
   halved, pounded thin (about
   2¹/₂ pounds)
¹/₂ cup butter or margarine
¹/₃ cup dry white wine
10 ounces angel hair pasta, hot
   cooked and drained
   Chopped fresh parsley

In small bowl, whisk together salad dressing and mustard; set aside. In medium skillet, sauté chicken in butter until tender and juices run clear. Remove from skillet; keep warm.

Pour wine into skillet; cook over medium-high heat, scraping up any browned bits from bottom of skillet, about 5 minutes. Whisk in dressing mixture; blend well. Serve chicken over pasta; top with sauce and sprinkle with parsley.   *Serves 8 as a main dish*

Dressed Chicken Breast with Angel Hair Pasta

Chicken with Fruit and Mixed Mustards

2 boneless skinless chicken breasts, halved (about 1¼ pounds)
½ cup Dijon-style mustard
½ cup Bavarian or other German mustard*
1 tablespoon Chinese mustard*
⅓ cup honey
⅓ cup light cream
½ teaspoon salt
¼ teaspoon pepper
2 tablespoons butter or margarine
4 kiwifruit, peeled and sliced
2 cups melon balls (honeydew and cantaloupe)
¼ cup mayonnaise
Mint sprigs for garnish

Combine mustards, honey and cream in medium bowl. Spoon half of mustard sauce into large glass bowl; reserve remaining mustard sauce. Sprinkle chicken with salt and pepper; place in glass bowl, turning to coat with mustard sauce. Cover; marinate in refrigerator 30 minutes, turning often.

Heat butter in large skillet over medium heat until foamy. Add chicken; cook about 7 minutes on each side or until chicken is tender and juices run clear. Remove chicken to cutting board; cut across grain into thin slices. Arrange chicken and fruit on serving platter.

Place reserved mustard sauce in small saucepan; whisk in mayonnaise. Heat thoroughly over medium heat. *Do not boil.* Drizzle some of the sauce over chicken. Garnish platter with mint sprigs. Pass remaining sauce.

Makes 4 servings

*German and Chinese mustards are made from brown mustard seed; their flavors are zestier than yellow prepared mustard. German and Chinese mustards can be found in some supermarkets and specialty food shops.

*Favorite recipe from **Delmarva Poultry Industry, Inc.***

Baked Chicken Breasts with Rice and Vegetable Stuffing

1 envelope LIPTON® Vegetable Recipe Soup Mix
1½ cups water
½ cup uncooked rice
1 package (10 ounces) frozen chopped spinach, cooked and squeezed dry
½ medium tomato, coarsely chopped
½ cup (2 ounces) shredded mozzarella cheese
¼ cup grated Parmesan cheese
1 small clove garlic, finely chopped
4 boneless skinless chicken breasts, halved (about 2½ pounds)
Paprika

In medium saucepan, blend vegetable recipe soup mix with water; bring to a boil over medium-high heat. Stir in rice; simmer, covered, 20 minutes or until tender. Stir in spinach, tomato, cheeses and garlic; set aside.

Preheat oven to 350°F. With knife parallel to cutting board, make deep, 3-inch cut in center of each chicken breast half to form pocket. Evenly stuff pockets with rice mixture.

In lightly greased baking dish, arrange chicken; bake, uncovered, basting occasionally, 40 minutes or until tender and juices run clear. Sprinkle with paprika.

Makes 8 servings

Chicken with Fruit and Mixed Mustards

Chicken Smothered in Roasted Garlic with Sweet Basil Red Gravy

Roasted Garlic (recipe follows)
2 cups vegetable or olive oil
1 broiler-fryer chicken, cut up
    (about 3 pounds)
2 tablespoons plus 4 teaspoons
    Chef Paul Prudhomme's
    POULTRY MAGIC®, divided
1 cup all-purpose flour
2 cups finely chopped onions
3 bay leaves
1 cup finely chopped green bell
    pepper
3½ cups peeled, chopped tomatoes
1 cup tomato sauce
3 tablespoons chopped fresh basil *or*
    1½ teaspoons dried basil leaves
2 tablespoons light brown sugar
3 cups skimmed chicken stock
    or water
½ teaspoon salt
    Hot cooked rice (preferably
    converted) or pasta

Prepare Roasted Garlic; reserve. Heat oil in large skillet over high heat. Season chicken with 1 tablespoon Poultry

Chicken Smothered in Roasted Garlic with Sweet Basil Red Gravy

Magic®. Blend flour and 2 teaspoons Poultry Magic® in another dish. Dust chicken pieces with seasoned flour. Add chicken pieces to hot oil (cook larger pieces first, skin side down); brown 3 to 4 minutes on each side. When browned (chicken should not be fully cooked), remove chicken pieces from skillet; drain on paper towels. Pour off all but ¼ cup oil. Reheat oil in skillet over high heat; add onions. Reduce heat to medium; add 2 teaspoons Poultry Magic® and bay leaves. Cook until onions are browned, stirring occasionally, about 5 minutes. Add bell pepper; cook 2 minutes.

Add tomatoes. Increase heat to high; cook 1 minute. Stir in tomato sauce and basil; cook about 1 minute. Add Roasted Garlic; cook about 1 minute. Stir in brown sugar; cook about 3 minutes. Add remaining 1 tablespoon Poultry Magic®; cook about 1 minute. Stir in stock. Return chicken pieces to skillet; bring to a boil. Simmer, uncovered, about 25 minutes or until chicken is tender and juices run clear, stirring occasionally to keep chicken from sticking. Add salt; cook about 1 minute. Remove and discard bay leaves before serving. Serve with rice or pasta. *Makes 4 servings*

Roasted Garlic

35 unpeeled garlic cloves (about
    2 large heads garlic)
Vegetable oil (Method 1 only)

Method 1: Submerge unpeeled garlic in oil heated to 350°F until outer skins begin to brown. Cool at room temperature; peel.

Method 2: Place unpeeled garlic on baking sheet or in shallow baking pan. Do not crowd. Bake in preheated 400°F oven until outer skins appear dry and edges begin to brown, 12 to 15 minutes. Cool at room temperature; peel.

Chicken Ragoût with Chilies, Tortillas and Goat Cheese

1 cup BLUE DIAMOND® Sliced
    Natural Almonds
6 tablespoons vegetable oil, divided
6 corn tortillas
2 boneless skinless chicken breasts,
    halved (about 1¼ pounds)
1 cup chicken stock or broth
1 onion, chopped
1 red bell pepper, cut into strips
1 can (7 ounces) whole green chilies,
    cut crosswise into ¼-inch strips
1½ teaspoons ground cumin
1 cup heavy cream
8 ounces goat cheese
1 tablespoon lime juice
½ to 1 teaspoon salt

Cook and stir almonds in 1 tablespoon oil over medium-high heat in small saucepan until golden; reserve. Heat 4 tablespoons oil; soften tortillas in oil, one at a time, about 30 seconds. Drain on paper towels and cut into ½-inch strips; reserve.

Poach chicken breasts, covered, in barely simmering chicken stock in medium saucepan about 10 minutes or just until tender and chicken is no longer pink in center. Remove chicken from stock; reserve stock. Slice chicken into strips. In large skillet, cook and stir onion and bell pepper in remaining 1 tablespoon oil until onion is translucent. Add chilies and cumin; cook and stir 1 minute. Stir in reserved chicken stock and cream; simmer 2 to 3 minutes. Add chicken. Stir in goat cheese; *do not boil.* Add lime juice and salt. Fold in reserved tortilla strips and almonds.

Makes 4 servings

Chicken Americana with Wisconsin Blue Cheese

4 ounces Wisconsin Blue cheese
1 package (3 ounces) cream cheese,
    softened
1 egg
3 tablespoons plain dry bread
    crumbs
2 tablespoons walnuts
1 tablespoon chopped fresh parsley
¼ teaspoon pepper
6 boneless skinless chicken breasts,
    pounded (about 3¾ pounds)
    All-purpose flour
    Butter

Cream cheeses until smooth in small bowl. Blend in egg, crumbs, walnuts, parsley and pepper. Place ⅓ cup cheese mixture on one half of each chicken breast. Roll up chicken to enclose filling completely; secure with wooden toothpicks.

Lightly dredge chicken rolls in flour. Melt butter over medium-high heat in large skillet. Sauté chicken rolls in butter until golden brown on all sides. Place chicken rolls in baking pan. Bake in 375°F oven 20 minutes or until chicken is tender and juices run clear. Remove chicken rolls; let stand 5 to 8 minutes. Slice and serve.

Makes 6 servings

Favorite recipe from Wisconsin Milk Marketing Board © 1992

Chicken and Vegetable Roll-Ups

1 large carrot, pared and cut into thin strips
1 red bell pepper, cut into thin strips
1 medium summer squash, cut into thin strips
1 medium zucchini, cut into thin strips
3 boneless skinless chicken breasts, split and pounded (about 2 pounds)
2 tablespoons vegetable oil
1 cup plus 2 tablespoons water
1 cup sliced fresh mushrooms
2 teaspoons WYLER'S® or STEERO® Chicken-Flavor Instant Bouillon *or* 2 Chicken-Flavor Bouillon Cubes
1 tablespoon cornstarch
2 tablespoons dry sherry, optional
1/2 teaspoon dried tarragon leaves
    Hot cooked rice

Place equal amounts of vegetables on each chicken breast half. Roll chicken around vegetables; secure with wooden toothpicks. In large skillet, brown roll-ups in oil. Add *1 cup* water, mushrooms and bouillon; bring to a boil. Reduce heat. Cover; simmer 15 minutes or until chicken is tender. Remove roll-ups from skillet. Combine remaining *2 tablespoons* water and cornstarch. Stir cornstarch mixture, sherry and tarragon into skillet; cook and stir until thickened. Spoon sauce over roll-ups and rice. Refrigerate leftovers.   *Makes 6 servings*

Laguna Beach Pecan Chicken Breasts

4 boneless skinless chicken breasts, halved (about 2 1/2 pounds)
    Pepper
6 tablespoons unsalted butter or vegetable oil
1/4 cup plus 2 tablespoons Dijon-style mustard, divided
2 cups pecan halves, finely ground
1 1/2 to 2 cups plain yogurt
1 cup California pitted ripe olives, sliced
1 package (1 ounce) HIDDEN VALLEY RANCH® Original Ranch® Salad Dressing Mix

Preheat oven to 400°F. Pound chicken breast halves between 2 pieces of plastic wrap to 1/4-inch thickness; season with pepper. Melt butter in small saucepan over low heat. Remove saucepan from heat; whisk in 1/4 cup mustard. (If using oil, whisk oil with 1/4 cup mustard in small bowl.) Dip chicken into mustard mixture; roll in ground pecans to coat evenly. Arrange chicken in single layer in lightly greased baking pan. Bake 15 minutes or until chicken is tender and juices run clear.

Meanwhile, thoroughly combine yogurt, olives, salad dressing mix and remaining 2 tablespoons mustard in medium saucepan. Remove chicken from baking pan. Stir pan drippings into yogurt mixture; simmer over low heat 2 minutes. Place 2 tablespoons yogurt sauce on each dinner plate; top with a chicken breast. Serve with remaining sauce. Garnish as desired.

Makes 8 servings

Laguna Beach Pecan Chicken Breast

Chicken Normandy with Noodles

Chicken Normandy with Noodles

2 boneless skinless chicken breasts,
   halved (about 1¼ pounds)
Salt and pepper
4 tablespoons butter or margarine,
   divided
¼ teaspoon dried thyme leaves
1 medium onion, chopped
1 large tart red apple, unpeeled and
   chopped
½ cup apple juice
2 tablespoons dry white wine
   (optional)
1½ cups water
½ cup milk
1 package LIPTON® Noodles &
   Sauce – Alfredo
2 tablespoons finely chopped fresh
   parsley
Pepper

Lightly season chicken with salt and pepper. In large skillet, melt 2 tablespoons butter; cook chicken and thyme over medium-high heat until chicken is lightly browned. Remove chicken from skillet; keep warm. Into same skillet, add onion and apple; cook until tender. Stir in apple juice and wine; simmer 2 minutes or until liquid is reduced by half. Return chicken to skillet; simmer, covered, 5 minutes or until chicken is tender and juices run clear.

Meanwhile, in medium saucepan, bring water, milk and remaining 2 tablespoons butter to a boil. Stir in noodles & alfredo sauce. Continue boiling over medium heat, stirring occasionally, 8 minutes or until noodles are tender. Stir in parsley; season with pepper to taste. To serve, arrange chicken and apple mixture over noodles. Garnish as desired.

Makes 4 servings

Chicken alla Vineyard

2 boneless chicken breasts, halved
  (about 1¼ pounds)
2 tablespoons all-purpose flour
½ teaspoon dried basil leaves,
  crushed
½ teaspoon salt
¼ teaspoon dried tarragon leaves,
  crushed
¼ teaspoon paprika
⅛ teaspoon white pepper
1 tablespoon vegetable oil
1 tablespoon butter
2 cloves garlic, minced
⅓ cup dry white wine
⅔ cup chicken broth
1 teaspoon lemon juice
1 cup imported winter red grape
  halves, seeded
1 tablespoon finely chopped fresh
  parsley

Remove skin from chicken, if desired.
Cut chicken breast halves lengthwise in
half. Combine flour, basil, salt,
tarragon, paprika and pepper. Coat
chicken with flour mixture; reserve
excess flour mixture. Heat oil and butter
in large skillet over medium-high heat.
Add chicken; cook until golden brown
on one side. Turn chicken; add garlic,
reserved flour mixture and wine. Cover;
cook 5 minutes. Add broth, lemon juice
and grapes. Cook, uncovered,
5 minutes or until chicken is tender and
juices run clear. Remove chicken and
grapes to heated serving platter. Boil
sauce 1 minute; pour over chicken.
Sprinkle with parsley.

Makes 4 servings

Favorite recipe from **Chilean Winter Fruit Association**

Mustard Chicken

1 broiler-fryer chicken, cut up and
  skinned (2½ to 3 pounds)
  Freshly ground pepper
½ cup prepared mustard*
2 tablespoons brown sugar
1 clove garlic, minced
½ teaspoon dry mustard
  Plain dry bread crumbs

Preheat oven to 400°F. Sprinkle chicken
pieces with pepper. Place on rack in
roasting pan; bake until lightly
browned, 10 to 15 minutes.

Combine prepared mustard, brown
sugar, garlic and dry mustard; blend
well. Brush both sides of chicken with
mustard mixture. Dip chicken into
crumbs to coat evenly. Place chicken on
rack in roasting pan; bake 20 minutes.
Turn chicken over; bake 30 minutes or
until chicken is tender and coating is
crunchy.   *Makes 4 to 6 servings*

*Substitute ¼ cup prepared mustard
mixed with ¼ cup Dijon-style mustard
for the prepared mustard.

Favorite recipe from **National Sugar Association, Inc.**

Mustard Chicken

Chicken Breasts Sautéed with Sun-Dried Tomatoes

4 boneless skinless chicken breasts, halved (about 2½ pounds)
8 to 10 sun-dried tomatoes*
1 container (15 ounces) POLLY-O® Ricotta cheese
1 package (4 ounces) POLLY-O® shredded Mozzarella cheese (1 cup)
⅓ cup POLLY-O® grated Parmesan or Romano cheese
1 egg, beaten
2 tablespoons chopped fresh parsley
½ teaspoon garlic powder
¼ teaspoon pepper
2 tablespoons pine nuts
2 tablespoons currants
⅓ cup butter or margarine
⅔ cup sliced shallots
1 cup chicken broth
½ cup dry white wine

Pound chicken breast halves between 2 pieces of plastic wrap to ¼-inch thickness. Chop enough tomatoes to measure ⅓ cup; slice remaining tomatoes into strips. Combine cheeses, egg, chopped tomatoes, parsley, garlic powder and pepper in medium bowl; blend well. Divide cheese mixture evenly between chicken breast halves; spread to within 1 inch of edges. Sprinkle with pine nuts and currants. Roll up chicken jelly-roll fashion; secure with wooden toothpicks to enclose filling entirely.

Melt butter in large skillet over medium-high heat; add chicken rolls. Cook chicken rolls until golden on all sides; remove from skillet and keep warm. Add shallots and tomato strips to skillet; cook and stir over low heat 2 minutes. Blend in broth and wine; cook 3 minutes. Return chicken to

Chicken Breasts Sautéed with Sun-Dried Tomatoes

skillet. Cover; simmer 15 to 20 minutes or until chicken is tender and juices run clear, basting several times and turning once. Garnish as desired.

Makes 8 servings

*Sun-dried tomatoes are available in some supermarkets and specialty shops. If unavailable, substitute 8 to 10 mushrooms.

Fruit Pesto with Chicken and Pasta

2 tubs (12 ounces each) OCEAN SPRAY® Cran-Fruit™ Crushed Fruit for Chicken
½ cup fresh basil leaves, loosely packed
½ cup chopped walnuts
¼ cup grated Parmesan cheese
¼ cup olive oil
1 pound chicken tenders
2 tablespoons vegetable oil
9 ounces hot cooked angel hair pasta, drained

To make pesto, place Cran-Fruit™ Crushed Fruit for Chicken, basil, walnuts and cheese in blender or food processor container. While processing, slowly add olive oil in thin stream until mixture thickens; set aside.

Cook chicken in vegetable oil in large skillet over medium-high heat until no longer pink in center and golden brown. Place chicken and pasta in large serving bowl. Stir in pesto, tossing gently until well mixed.

Makes 4 servings

Coconut Chicken with Fresh Chutney

Coconut Chicken with Fresh Chutney

1 (15-ounce) can COCO LOPEZ®
    Cream of Coconut
3 cups chopped nectarines or apples
½ cup raisins
½ lemon, seeded and chopped
    (about ¼ cup)
⅓ cup firmly packed light brown
    sugar
¼ cup apple cider vinegar
1 tablespoon finely chopped fresh
    ginger root
½ teaspoon curry powder
1 clove garlic, finely chopped
¼ cup flaked coconut
2 tablespoons soy sauce
2 whole chicken breasts, split *or*
    8 chicken thighs

Reserve ¾ *cup* cream of coconut; set aside. Combine nectarines, raisins, lemon, sugar, vinegar, ginger, curry powder and garlic in medium saucepan; mix well. Bring to a boil. Boil 2 minutes, stirring occasionally. Cool. Add flaked coconut and remaining cream of coconut; mix well. Cover chutney; refrigerate overnight to allow flavors to blend.

Preheat oven to 350°F. Combine reserved ¾ *cup* cream of coconut and soy sauce. Arrange chicken pieces in 12×8-inch baking dish; pour coconut mixture over top. Bake 45 minutes to 1 hour or until tender, basting frequently. Serve chicken with chutney. Garnish as desired.   *Makes 4 servings*

Chicken Macadamia

6 boneless skinless chicken breasts
(about 3³⁄₄ pounds)
1 cup plus 1 tablespoon dry
champagne
4¹⁄₂ teaspoons butter
2¹⁄₂ tablespoons all-purpose flour
¹⁄₂ cup chicken stock or broth
¹⁄₄ cup heavy cream
1¹⁄₂ teaspoons chopped fresh parsley
Dash freshly ground pepper
2¹⁄₂ cups (10 ounces) shredded
Wisconsin Sharp Cheddar
cheese, divided
¹⁄₂ cup macadamia nuts, toasted and
chopped*

Pound chicken breasts to ¹⁄₄-inch
thickness. Place in large pan; cover with
1 cup champagne. Marinate, covered,
2 hours.

Melt butter over low heat. Stir in flour
until smooth. Gradually add chicken
stock and cream to butter mixture.
Cook until smooth and thickened,
stirring constantly. Add remaining
1 tablespoon champagne, parsley and
pepper. Sauce should be fairly thin.

Remove chicken from marinade; discard
marinade. Combine cheese and nuts.
Sprinkle ¹⁄₃ to ¹⁄₂ cup in center of each
chicken breast. Roll up chicken, tucking
in sides, and place, seam side down, on
baking sheet. Pour half of sauce over
chicken rolls; reserve remaining sauce.

Bake at 325°F, 45 minutes or until
chicken is tender and juices run clear.
Place chicken rolls on plates. Spoon
remaining sauce and any melted cheese
filling from baking pan over chicken
rolls. Garnish with additional toasted
macadamia nuts and chopped fresh
parsley, if desired.   *Makes 6 servings*

*To toast macadamia nuts, spread nuts
in shallow pan. Bake in preheated 350°F
oven 12 to 15 minutes or until golden
brown, stirring frequently.

*Favorite recipe from **Wisconsin Milk Marketing
Board** © 1992*

Chicken Macadamia

Acknowledgments

The publishers would like to thank the companies and organizations listed below for the use of their recipes in this publication.

American Dairy Association
American Spice Trade Association
Best Foods, a Division of CPC International Inc.
Blue Diamond Growers
Borden Kitchens, Borden, Inc.
California Apricot Advisory Board
California Avocado Commission
California Table Grape Commission
California Tree Fruit Agreement
Carnation, Nestlé Food Company
Chef Paul Prudhomme's Magic Seasoning
  Blends™
Chilean Winter Fruit Association
Contadina Foods, Inc., Nestlé Food Company
The Creamette Company
Delmarva Poultry Industry, Inc.
Del Monte Corporation
Dole Food Company, Inc.
Durkee-French Foods, A Division of Reckitt &
  Colman Inc.
Filippo Berio Olive Oil
Florida Department of Citrus
The Fresh Garlic Association

Heinz U.S.A.
The HVR Company
Kellogg Company
Kikkoman International Inc.
Kraft General Foods, Inc.
Lawry's® Foods, Inc.
Thomas J. Lipton Co.
McIlhenny Company
Nabisco Foods Group
National Broiler Council
Nestlé Specialty Products Company
New York Cherry Growers Association, Inc.
Ocean Spray Cranberries, Inc.
Pace Foods, Inc.
Pet Incorporated
Pollio Dairy Products
The Procter & Gamble Company, Inc.
The Quaker Oats Company
The Sugar Association, Inc.
Uncle Ben's Rice
USA Rice Council
Walnut Marketing Board
Wisconsin Milk Marketing Board

Photo Credits

The publishers would like to thank the companies and organizations listed below for the use of their photographs in this publication.

Best Foods, a Division of CPC International Inc.
Borden Kitchens, Borden, Inc.
California Apricot Advisory Board
Carnation, Nestlé Food Company
Chef Paul Prudhomme's Magic Seasoning
  Blends™
Contadina Foods, Inc., Nestlé Food Company
The Creamette Company
Del Monte Corporation
Dole Food Company, Inc.
Heinz U.S.A.

The HVR Company
Kikkoman International Inc.
Kraft General Foods, Inc.
Lawry's® Foods, Inc.
Thomas J. Lipton Co.
McIlhenny Company
National Broiler Council
The Quaker Oats Company
Uncle Ben's Rice
USA Rice Council
Wisconsin Milk Marketing Board

INDEX